THE LOST ART OF
MEDITATION

THE LOST ART OF
MEDITATION

DEEPENING YOUR PRAYER LIFE

SHEILA PRITCHARD

Scripture Union, 207–209 Queensway, Bletchley, MK2 2EB,
England, UK.
Email: info@scriptureunion.org.uk
website: www.scriptureunion.org.uk

British Library Cataloguing-in-Publication Data
A catalogue record for this book is available from the British Library.

Cover design and chapter heads by Kessell Design Consultants.

Printed and bound in Great Britain by Creative Print and Design (Wales)
Ebbw Vale

Scripture Union is an international Christian charity working with
churches in more than 130 countries, providing resources to bring the good
news about Jesus Christ to children, young people and families and to
encourage them to develop spiritually through the Bible and prayer.
As well as our network of volunteers, staff and associates who run holidays,
church-based events and school Christian groups, we produce a wide range
of publications and support those who use our resources through training
programmes.

Chapter 4

1 'Shells' by Joy Cowley, from *Aotearoa Psalms*, catholic.supplies@clear.net.nz

2 Sheila Hocken, *Emma and I*, Sphere Books, 1978

Chapter 5

1 *The Practice of the Presence of God; Being Conversations and letters of Brother Lawrence* (London: Epworth Press 1959) © Trustees for Methodist Church Purposes. Used by permission of the Methodist Publishing House

2 James Houston, *The Transforming Friendship*, Lion Publishing 1989

for Anthea
with whom I share the experience that:
'Love consists in this, that two solitudes protect and touch
and greet each other.'
Ranier Maria Rilke

CONTENTS

PREFACE

Most of us don't like to admit that prayer sometimes feels like a duty, an obligation – and rather hard work! We imagine that everyone else has a wonderfully rich prayer life which is inspiring, uplifting and life-changing. So, very often, we keep quiet about what is actually going on (or not going on!) in our own relationship with God.

I was fortunate to be brought up in a Christian home where prayer was an integral part of life. We had family devotions every day. Reading the Bible with the aid of Scripture Union notes was part of my daily routine from childhood. My earliest memories are of knowing that God loved me, that Jesus was my friend and that I could talk to God whenever I wanted to. I'm grateful for such a wonderful foundation for life.

By the time I had completed Bible college training and served as a missionary in Nigeria for six years, you might expect I had prayer pretty well figured out! But that was the very time when I was the one not admitting that prayer felt like a dry duty and wondering if there was more to it than I had so far discovered. And of course there was! Some of what I have explored since then is included in this book.

My own pilgrimage in prayer soon became a passion I wanted to share with others. I have had the privilege of spending about fifteen years teaching spirituality at the Bible College of New Zealand and accompanying many people individually on their spiritual journeys. Now I know without doubt that there are many others who, like me, come to a season in prayer where they wonder if there's 'more to it than I've so far discovered'. Realising this is not a guilty secret to be kept hidden, but a wonderful desire to motivate exploration!

So this is a book for people who are bored with prayer. It's for faithful pray-ers who know in the depth of their being that prayer matters, but who secretly wish there was more life to it.

This is a book for those who long to explore creative, two-way communication with the amazing God of the universe. It's for those who have a desire to plumb the depths and enough holy daring to experiment.

This is a book for those who love the familiar, well-read scriptures but wish they could seem fresh and new again. It's for those who want to stay close to Jesus while discovering new paths to travel.

This is a book for those who want to live their prayer in their bodies, in action, in creation – as well as in their heads and hearts!

It really doesn't matter whether you think of yourself as a beginner or a seasoned traveller. When it comes to prayer, we are all beginners in some new aspect of the journey. I suggest you browse this book and see if it invites you into areas you want to explore. If it does, settle in and journey!

❧

CHAPTER 1
Planted by the water

> *'Blessed are those who trust in the Lord, whose trust is the Lord. They shall be like a tree planted by water, sending out its roots by the stream. It shall not fear when heat comes, and its leaves shall stay green; in the year of drought it is not anxious, and it does not cease to bear fruit.'* (Jeremiah 17:7,8)

> *'Happy are those who do not follow the advice of the wicked, or take the path that sinners tread, or sit in the seat of scoffers; but their delight is in the law of the Lord, and on his law they meditate day and night. They are like trees planted by streams of water, which yield their fruit in its season, and their leaves do not wither. In all that they do, they prosper. The wicked are not so, but are like chaff that the wind drives away. Therefore the wicked will not stand in the judgement, nor sinners in the congregation of the righteous; for the Lord watches over the way of the righteous, but the way of the wicked will perish.'* (Psalm 1)

Wouldn't it be marvellous to be in constant contact with the never ending stream of God's abundant life? Imagine having no concern at all about running dry or running out of spiritual nourishment. Picture a life of steady fruitfulness – progressing through the seasons, obviously – but always in the flow of producing healthy fruit.

Does it all seem too good to be true? Do such ideas engender excitement at the possibility, or frustration because such a lifestyle seems out of reach? Whatever your initial reaction, you are not alone! The Christian life is full of mystery. Things that sound simple on a first reading don't seem to work out that way in experience. Then we're left with niggling questions: Did I miss something? Am I not 'doing it right'? Perhaps the Bible doesn't mean what it seems to mean. Am I the only one who isn't experiencing the spiritual high that others speak of?

Meet some travelling companions

Let me introduce you to some people I know. In one sense none of these people really exists, in another sense they all do! Of course I have changed names and details, but every circumstance and issue is real.

There's Fran, mother of two teenagers, and faithful volunteer for church and community activities. She turned forty recently and was given two Bibles for her birthday. She already has more than one Bible and is known as a committed Bible reader. Neither of her friends knew the other was giving her a Bible. They had each chosen one from the vast range of Bibles on sale these days – one was a Women's Study Bible and the other an inclusive language New International Version. In different ways both friends told her that because she was such a committed Christian, they thought a new Bible would be the gift she'd most appreciate. Telling me about it she smiled rather wistfully as she admitted that though she is currently carrying out a programme of reading the Bible in a year, she feels that God is far away and her reading is a rather dry duty. As we talked further, it became clear that for many years she has longed to have a relationship with God that felt loving and life-giving, but somehow it never seems to happen.

Brendan is a theological college student training for the ministry. His background in a charismatic church has given him a firm foundation in the evangelical gospel, the centrality of the Bible, the gifts of the Spirit and the power of prayer. But suddenly, in the face of critical scholarship, a wide range of theological points of view and so many people who see things differently, he doesn't know what to believe any more or how to pray. He agonises over the fact that he is supposed to be training to lead others on their Christian journey but he feels more confused than ever before.

Maisie is both sad and angry. Both are very hard to admit. After all, when you've been a Christian for forty-five years and prayed and served faithfully all of that time, it is hard to face that you feel God has done wonderful things for others but somehow left you feeling drained and empty. 'Surely after all these years I should know all the right answers about spiritual vibrancy? So how come I feel they don't work for me?'

Pat is a very successful career woman whom others admire. She has headed up two para-church organisations, moving from one to the next with high commendation from previous employers. She has always felt that her purpose in life was to serve God, and leading Christian organisations seemed to be the way for her to do that. The trouble is she is so busy that prayer hardly gets a look in. She often asks God for help in the midst of a difficult situation, and of course she leads staff devotions when it's her turn. But she feels vaguely guilty that in the high-pressured whirl of Christian service there isn't really any energy left for 'quality time with God'.

Robin calls himself a plodder. When he commits himself to something, he sticks with it steadily and faithfully. He values that about himself, and others do too. 'If you ask Robin to do something, you know it will be done and done well.' He's faithfully stayed on the spiritual journey too. Rarely does he miss his regular time for Bible reading and prayer. He follows a Bible reading pattern with helpful notes and has a prayer diary with the names of family, friends, missionaries, local and world needs listed for each day. He's rather hesitant about broaching the subject, but finally he wonders aloud if maybe there is something missing. He's quick to add that maybe there's not. Perhaps this is just how it's supposed to be, and if so he's happy to continue his routine. After all, prayer is not about feeling good – that would be very self-centred. But he does just wonder if there could be more to it than he's so far discovered.

I wonder what happened in you as you read these stories. Were you shocked, or did you identify with someone?

Don't walk past the signpost!

I chose these people because they are all longing to be 'like a tree planted by the water' with the qualities that the scriptures say go with that. They might not put it in those words, but that is the deep desire of each one. They are not failures or 'backsliding', nor are they treating their Christian faith lightly. On the contrary, they are willing to be honest and to give priority to exploring their questions. Honesty and openness are two of the most important foundations for a deepening prayer journey, so each of these people is well on the way.

The readings from Jeremiah and Psalm 1 give two significant

pointers as to what enables people to be like trees planted by streams of water. They can be expressed so briefly that we might almost miss them: trust in the Lord and meditate on his Word. That doesn't sound particularly revolutionary! Almost any Christian would agree that you can't get far without trusting God, and of course God's Word is important so we need to read it and think about it. So what's new? What's new for many is that trustful, meditative prayer is unexplored territory. It is as if we have walked past the sign pointing to the underground spring where the water flows, and have never taken the track right down into the depths.

Prayer is a vast arena with many aspects to explore. In this book we are going to focus on deepening the roots of our prayer life. To do this we will focus on the more meditative aspects of prayer. We'll explore ways of praying that take us down deep into the living water of God's Word and prayer that enables the life-giving presence of God to spring up in the midst of our busy everyday life. Other aspects of prayer like intercession, confession, petition, adoration and thanksgiving are important too, but they have books of their own! One of the key features of meditative prayer is that it is more about listening than talking. It's more about taking in what God is saying than making sure he hears what I'm saying. That in itself can be quite a turnaround. One of the most common views about prayer is that it is primarily about talking to God – and of course that's part of it – but all too often it becomes a one-way conversation. When that happens, the roots of our tree stop drinking from the water, and we start to dry up, becoming tired, cynical, angry or bored, or maybe just faithfully plodding on thinking this is all there is.

What's up ahead?

If you identify with any of the people I introduced earlier, learning new and creative ways of meditative prayer will open up new possibilities. For example:

● Letting one tiny little 'seed' from scripture take root in the depth of your being and quietly grow in secret until it flowers in a surprising way.

- Finding yourself interacting with Jesus in a Gospel story so that it becomes your own story right here and now.

- Discovering that prayerful meditation can be done on the move, out in creation, as well as in the stillness of your room.

- Developing the art of incorporating prayer into even the busiest day.

- Exploring creative, non-verbal ways of praying when words fail.

- Enjoying the freedom to pray in a way that suits your personality.

These are all ways of letting your roots grow deeply into the streams of water that will nourish the tree of your life and sustain it whatever the weather!

Looking at the big picture

Before we start exploring each of those ways in detail, let's take a 'big picture' look at what meditation is from a biblical perspective. In the Old Testament meditation is regarded as an essential aspect of godly living. The Israelites were to ensure that God's word was repeatedly recalled and remembered in every aspect of daily life.

> *'Fix these words of mine in your hearts and minds; tie them as symbols on your hands and bind them on your foreheads. Teach them to your children, talking about them when you sit at home and when you walk along the road, when you lie down and when you get up. Write them on the door-frames of your houses and on your gates, so that your days and the days of your children may be many in the land that the Lord swore to give your forefathers, as many as the days that the heavens are above the earth.' (Deuteronomy 11:18–21, NIV)*

In more contemporary language it seems to me that God is saying: 'My words are your source of life, so soak yourself in them in every way you can. This will involve your heart as well as your mind. Use various kinds of symbols as powerful reminders. Ordinary conversations will help you chew over the implications of my words to daily life. You can ponder them as you walk and write them down so you don't forget. My words will restore you as you lie down to rest and motivate you as you get up to face the new day. Use all these ways to draw life from me so that your days will be full and fruitful.'

That is a pretty comprehensive description of what biblical meditation can cover! This passage in Deuteronomy puts into practical terms what Psalm 1 describes in a symbolic picture. Making sure the roots of our tree go down into the life-giving water means actually practising meditation on a daily basis. How to do that is what this book is about.

Joshua is a biblical character who put to the test the fruits of meditation. When he faced the daunting task of leading the Israelites into the Promised Land, Joshua was told that the key to his success would be his practice of meditation.

> 'Be strong and courageous because you will lead these people to inherit the land I swore to their forefathers to give them. Be strong and very courageous. Be careful to obey all the law my servant Moses gave you; do not turn from it to the right or to the left, that you may be successful wherever you go. Do not let this Book of the Law depart from your mouth; meditate on it day and night, so that you may be careful to do everything written in it. Then you will be prosperous and successful. Have I not commanded you? Be strong and courageous. Do not be terrified; do not be discouraged, for the Lord your God will be with you wherever you go.'
> (Joshua 1:6–9, NIV)

If you faced an extremely challenging and risky task and were told there was a key to handling it well, I'm sure you would be eager to find out exactly what that key was and how to use it! Of course the truth is that we are all facing the risky task of living life. Every day there are challenges. No life is free of risk, hard decisions, disappointments, surprises and situations that stretch our ability to cope.

You may not be leading a whole nation into a promised land, but you are invited to walk into God's promised land for you. For you, just as for Joshua, a key to facing life's challenges well is meditation on God's Word, so that it becomes a part of the very fibre of your being as you move forward courageously.

The best example of a person whose life showed the fruit of meditation is Jesus. His Jewish heritage would have ensured that as a child and an adult he was immersed in the Hebrew scriptures. He would have lived in the way described in Deuteronomy. Even as a twelve-year-old he astounded the rabbis with his wisdom. Later, in the supreme challenge of his temptations (see Matthew 4), the scriptures which were deeply ingrained in him were the key to his ability to stay true to his call. There was no time in the moment of testing to go off and consult others or look up the answer in the back of the book! The years of meditation meant that the word was there at hand to meet the challenge. Even in the dryness and drought of the desert, the living water from deep inner springs ensured that Jesus did not wither.

Jesus shows us too that meditation needs to be current and contemporary. It is not only about recalling God's words in the past, although that is a very important aspect as we have seen, but also about meditating on what God is saying to us now in our current situation. Jesus often did this by looking around and pointing out to his followers some aspect of creation or some everyday event and showing how this spoke of God.

'Therefore I tell you, do not worry about your life, what you will eat or drink; or about your body, what you will wear. Is not life more important than food, and the body more important than clothes? Look at the birds of the air; they do not sow or reap or store away in barns, and yet your heavenly Father feeds them. Are you not much more valuable than they? Who of you by worrying can add a single hour to his life? And why do you worry about clothes? See how the lilies of the field grow. They do not labour or spin. Yet I tell you that not even Solomon in all his splendour was dressed like one of these. If that is how God clothes the grass of the field, which is here today and tomorrow is thrown into the fire, will he not much more clothe you, O you of little faith? So do not worry, saying, "What shall we eat?" or "What shall we drink?" or "What shall we wear?" For the pagans run after all these things; and your heavenly Father knows that you need

*them. But seek first his kingdom and his righteousness, and all these things
will be given to you as well. Therefore do not worry about tomorrow, for
tomorrow will worry about itself. Each day has enough trouble of its own.'
(Matthew 6:25–34, NIV)*

If you had been there in the fields as Jesus spoke these words, I guess
you would have gone on pondering that message every time you saw
lilies in a field and birds flying by. Over and over again Jesus turned
people's attention to creation as a way of seeing more of what God
is like. He modelled for his followers the truth expressed in Romans
1:20: 'For since the creation of the world God's invisible qualities –
his eternal power and divine nature – have been clearly seen, being
understood from what has been made, so that we are without
excuse' (NIV). God's character as seen in creation is a rich source of
Christian meditation.

Another example is something as ordinary as a woman sweeping
her house to find a lost coin (Luke 15:8–10). Jesus turned a simple,
everyday event into a reminder of God's delight in seeking and finding a lost person. It seems that for Jesus everything could be used to
direct our minds to God.

Meditating on a truth is more than just hearing it once. It is discovering that the word takes root and keeps coming back with new
levels of meaning. Jesus' mother Mary knew how to do this. In Luke
2:19 we are told that in the events of Jesus' birth she 'treasured up
all these things and pondered them in her heart' (NIV). And twelve
years later it was still true: 'His mother treasured all these things in
her heart' (Luke 2:51). Treasuring God's word in our hearts is another good way to describe meditation. God's word may come to us
through the Scriptures, through God's creation and through God's
activity in our lives. The Holy Spirit uses all these ways to teach us,
remind us and lead us to the truth (John 14:16,17,26).

Clearing the ground

Meditative prayer is about actually following the sign that leads to
the deep underground springs of living water. Sometimes, however

much we like the sound of the destination, there are obstacles that make it hard to get started. One of these obstacles may be a vague distrust of the very word 'meditation'.

I hope it is clear already that Christian meditation is deeply rooted in biblical history and practice. However, meditation is also a discipline used by people of other faiths and in some secular settings, eg stress management seminars, some 'New Age' philosophies, etc. This makes some contemporary Christians wary of the very word meditation and questions arise as to how 'Christian' such an activity can be. By beginning with the biblical background to Christian meditation, I hope we have begun by laying a firm foundation in our own heritage. It is very sad when something which is deeply part of the Christian tradition gets lost by disuse or avoided because of fear, and Christians become more aware of the practices of other traditions than of their own.

It is interesting that almost every religious tradition has its forms of meditation. There is something every culture and race has discovered about entering deeply into what matters most to them. The difference is not so much in the practice of meditation but in the content of 'what it is that matters most'. For Christians, what matters most is the Word of God and the person of Jesus. The journey I invite you to travel with me is one which reclaims the riches of Christian meditation: entering deeply into the Word of God and the character of Jesus.

٭ Try it

As we conclude this introductory chapter, I invite you to read the following psalm slowly and reflect on the questions which follow.

> [1] *The heavens are telling the glory of God;*
> *and the firmament proclaims his handiwork.*
> [2] *Day to day pours forth speech,*
> *and night to night declares knowledge.*
> [3] *There is no speech, nor are there words;*
> *their voice is not heard;*
> [4] *yet their voice goes out through all the earth,*

and their words to the end of the world.

In the heavens he has set a tent for the sun,
5 *which comes out like a bridegroom from his wedding canopy,*
       and like a strong man runs its course with joy.
6 *Its rising is from the end of the heavens,*
       and its circuit to the end of them;
       and nothing is hid from its heat.
7 *The law of the Lord is perfect,*
       reviving the soul;
     the decrees of the Lord are sure,
       making wise the simple;
8 *the precepts of the Lord are right,*
       rejoicing the heart;
     the commandment of the Lord is clear,
       enlightening the eyes;
9 *the fear of the Lord is pure,*
       enduring forever;
     the ordinances of the Lord are true
       and righteous altogether.
10 *More to be desired are they than gold,*
       even much fine gold;
     sweeter also than honey,
       and drippings of the honeycomb.

11 *Moreover by them is your servant warned;*
       in keeping them there is great reward.
12 *But who can detect their errors?*
       Clear me from hidden faults.
13 *Keep back your servant also from the insolent;*
       do not let them have dominion over me.
     Then I shall be blameless,
       and innocent of great transgression.

14 *Let the words of my mouth and the meditation of my heart*
       be acceptable to you,
       O Lord, my rock and my redeemer.
     (Psalm 19)

- Notice how the psalmist sees creation as 'speaking' of God, yet without words (vs 1–4).

- Reflect on the symbols the psalmist uses to try to express what he experiences (vs 4–6).

- What symbolic or pictorial way would *you* choose to express your experience of creation?

- From verses 7–11 pick out the specific effects of meditating on God's Word. You could write them down beginning: 'If I meditate on God's Word it will (for example) revive my soul'.

- What other fruit of meditation is suggested by verses 12 and 13?

- The psalmist's final prayer is in verse 14. How would you like to express to God your desires as you set out on the journey of meditative prayer?

CHAPTER 2
Reviving the soul, rejoicing the heart

In the whirlwind pace of our sophisticated, electronic, Western lifestyle, how much we long to be revived and to recapture heartfelt joy as promised in Psalm 19. It seems that the more devices we have to make life easier, eg computers, the internet and mobile phones, the more stretched and frantic we become. Revived souls and rejoicing hearts are a wistful wish. Maybe in the holidays when I have time to stop...

Yet just a moment away God beckons. Slow down. Change gear. Pause. Listen. I want to revive your soul. There are treasures here to rejoice your heart.

One of the earliest ways of meditating on scripture is so simple that it is easy to miss its profound impact. I sometimes say half-jokingly that it is summed up in two road signs: 'Slow' and 'Stop'. In other words, read the biblical passage slowly until some word or phrase attracts your attention and then stop. Don't rush on. Let God speak. In many ways it is as simple as that, yet there are deep riches to be more fully explored. I'm referring to what the early Christians called *Lectio Divina* or holy reading.

Holy reading is a way of letting the heart of God touch your heart. It is about creating space for a heart-to-heart conversation triggered by the Word of God. A sixth-century Benedictine monk, Abbot Marmion, expressed it beautifully this way: 'We read under the eye of God until the heart is touched and leaps to flame.' In that simple sentence the pathway to the richly reviving effect of God's Word is laid out.

To make it easier to tread that path, Lectio Divina has been explained in four steps: reading (*lectio*), meditating (*meditatio*), praying (*oratio*) and contemplating (*contemplatio*). At once it is obvious that each phase of the process deserves careful attention.

Reading receptively

Holy reading is different from most of the other reading we do. With the welter of information available to us in books, newspapers, emails, the internet, billboards and TV, many of us have developed the survival mechanism of speed reading or skimming. We want to glean the essential facts and discard the rest as quickly as possible. While that may make good sense in coping with daily life, it definitely does not aid holy reading!

When we come to meditate on a passage of scripture, we are making a welcoming space for an encounter with the heart of God. Reading slowly and with anticipation heightens our awareness of the word, phrase or idea the Spirit may be beckoning us to notice. Reading quickly with our familiar goal-oriented 'get to the end of the passage' mentality, means that all too often we run right past the soul-reviving treasure being offered.

If the word of God for you on a given day is in the first verse you read, one verse is enough! To hasten on is like saying, 'I'm sorry, I haven't time to stop and hear what you have to say.' Silly, isn't it, when I put it like that? But old habits die hard, and reading slowly and being willing to stop at the Spirit's prompting is often a radically new approach.

When I teach groups of people this way of meditating on scripture, I often use Psalm 23 as the passage to read. That means I've meditated on Psalm 23 many times myself. I know the psalm by heart. I can rattle it off from beginning to end in a few seconds. I could say to myself, 'There's nothing new here.' But when I come to it, expecting to hear God's word to me on this particular day, there is always something new! I remember once being stopped by the word 'my' in the phrase 'the Lord is my shepherd'. It was significant that day because I was feeling stressed and rather resentful that all my energy was going into 'feeding God's sheep', and there seemed to be no nourishment for me. It was refreshing and soul-restoring to be reminded that God was *my* shepherd, not just everybody else's!

On another occasion I got no further than the phrase 'I shall not want'. There was something about that phrase that got under my skin. It both irritated and attracted me. I wanted to argue with God about it and at the same time I wanted to believe the truth it promised. When we read 'under the eye of God', the Spirit of God draws our attention to what is most fruitful to notice. Sometimes that call to stop and take note is attractive and heart-warming. Sometimes we squirm and want to avoid taking a deeper look. Hopefully, in either case, we have the wisdom and courage to stop and listen.

On the occasions I've just mentioned, the place to stop was clear immediately and I had no need to read on. It isn't always like that. Sometimes you may read slowly to the end of the psalm or chosen passage with nothing 'leaping off the page'. In that case read the passage again, now that you have the whole context in mind. Sometimes it takes a second or third reading before the gentle nudging of the Spirit is noticed.

In some of the early monastic traditions before people had individual copies of the Bible, the community would sit and listen as the passage for the day was slowly read aloud over and over again. When each person 'heard' their word for that day, they would quietly leave and go to their cell to continue their meditation. I imagine that some would leave after the first reading, and others would let the words wash over them many times before choosing the place to dwell more deeply.

Meditating reflectively

When the place to dwell more deeply is identified, we flow naturally into meditation. Instead of rushing on we pause, holding the word reverently in our mind and heart like an unwrapped gift. Meditating is like unwrapping the gift.

The metaphor of unwrapping a gift brings to mind several people I know who unwrap gifts in a variety of ways.

- At a family Christmas party, two-year-old Luke ran around excitedly saying, 'Look what I got!' waving his *still wrapped* gift for all to see! The package and the coloured paper distracted him from finding out what was inside.

- Personally I tend to rip into the paper and packaging quickly, keen to get to whatever is hidden within. I'll tidy up the strewn bits and pieces later!

- A good friend to whom I have given many gifts, has a different approach. She takes the package in her hands and turns it around, admiring the paper and ribbon. She shakes it, smells it, assesses its shape and weight and has fun guessing what it might contain. Then carefully she unties the ribbon and unsticks the Sellotape. The wrapping paper is taken off slowly and folded for recycling. With anticipation rising, she finally opens the last layer and savours the uncovered present delighting in every detail. It is very satisfying to give a gift to such a friend!

Meditating on God's Word is like exploring his gift slowly, carefully and with anticipation. It is about unwrapping the layers of significance one by one. This can be helped by asking reflective questions: Why did this particular phrase attract my attention? What pictures or images or associations do I have with this idea? How does this verse relate to my life right now? What might God be wanting me to see that I haven't seen before? If this phrase is uncomfortable for me, what is the challenge here?

I'm not suggesting that these questions should be asked mechanically like some sort of comprehension test. In fact meditation is a relaxed, free-flowing pondering of the Word. It is a way of loosening the soil of your soul so that the first tiny seed of a word or idea has the chance to grow and flower.

Recently I was meditating on Isaiah 42:1–9. I read the whole passage, noting wonderful images about how God's servant would not break the bruised reed or quench the dimly burning wick. I noted the promise that God is doing new things and former things have passed away. Plenty to meditate on! Yet for me that day as I read 'under the eye of God', the sentence that touched my heart was in verse 6: 'I have taken you by the hand and kept you.' I held that gift reverently and turned it over in my mind, exploring its richness. It was true, not only for the people Isaiah was addressing, but for me too. God has taken me by the hand and kept me. I let my mind wander back through my life's journey, noticing times of particular need or danger when God had indeed kept me. I found myself picturing the Lord standing beside me, holding my hand and saying: 'I will continue to be with you for richer for poorer, in sickness and in health, and even death will never part us!' I realised that God was reminding me of this truth again now because of two difficult decisions I was about to make. The seed of one sentence of God's Word took root and grew.

Prayerfully responding

You can probably tell that meditating and responding go together and often intermingle. Just as my friend unwraps her gifts with comments, questions and delight at every layer, so the unwrapping of meditation draws forth a response. In my experience with Isaiah 42:6, I was responding to God with gratitude, reminiscing with him about past events, feeling a sense of awe about the relevance of this word right now, expressing my desire to trust this promise in a new way. Many prayerful responses were woven into our meditative conversation. Holy reading has its own rhythm directed by the Spirit. At first we may need to check that we've moved through all the steps, a bit like counting time when learning a new piano piece. But soon the music takes over and the rhythm of the Spirit conducts our prayerful dance.

The significant thing about prayer in the meditation process is that it is our *response* to the word of God. It is not our shopping list of requests. It does not begin with our agenda. First we listen. Then we let the word take root and reveal its beauty or its challenge. Only then are we ready to respond prayerfully. We let God have his rightful place as the initiator of the conversation. And maybe our response is not always in words. Talking is only one way of praying. When met by the living God, biblical characters sometimes fell down in awestruck silence, or took off their shoes and worshipped. The psalmists let us know that sometimes tears are their prayer. David sang and danced to express both sorrow and joy. In his letter to the Romans, Paul assures us that even our deep, wordless sighs are a response the Spirit can interpret. When God's Word touches our heart, responses are many and varied. It is important to recognise them all as prayer.

Contemplatively resting

There comes a point when the conversation has a natural ending, when all our ways of responding are not enough to express the deepest longings of our heart. It is time to enter the silent resting place of contemplation. This can be as simple as sitting quietly for a few more minutes, just letting your spirit soak in the awareness of God's presence. It is letting yourself relax into the arms of love without words, without striving, without anything to *do*, just *being*.

Sometimes the contemplative place feels satisfyingly exhausting! It's like a runner crossing a finish line and relishing lying down on the grass, letting every muscle relax. Our meditation and response can be both exhilarating and challenging, and there comes a time for a resting place where all our thinking and pondering cease.

Some describe the contemplative place as one of velvety darkness. We enter the mystery of the God we can never contain within our thoughts or images. Abbot Marmion chooses an almost opposite image, describing it as one's heart 'leaping to flame'. Struggling to describe contemplation is not nearly so important as entering this experience for yourself. Resist the temptation to hurry on as soon as some insight has been gained in meditation. Surrender to the Giver of the gift in silent, trustful wonder.

Getting started

As I said earlier, in one way this method of prayerful meditation is as simple as 'Go slow' or 'Stop'. Yet for many of the people I talk to, the biggest problem is getting started! Remember some of the people I introduced in chapter 1? There's Fran, who reads many chapters of the Bible each day to make sure she gets through it in a year, but often finds it lifeless and boring. And Pat, who is so busy in her Christian ministry that time to sit quietly and make space for meditation is such a daunting thought that she never starts. Even Brendan, who spends all day studying the Bible for his degree, says he feels a strange resistance to moving from studying it to praying with it.

Each of these people is encountering the same obstacle, which has many faces. It is the basic resistance we humans have to meeting God at any depth. We want to and we don't want to at the same time! We reach forward with one foot and step back with the other. Our hearts long for intimacy – and fear what it might mean. We want God's light to shine on us, yet there are things we would rather keep hidden. The paradox runs deep in our conscious and unconscious mind. One friend put it this way: 'I just have to get over the hump. Once I do that, I'm so glad I did.' I know what she means. The place I usually go to, to meditate and pray, is a room downstairs. Quite often I am tempted to convince myself there are many things I need to do today and prayer can wait. When that happens I have to make a conscious choice to walk down the stairs, into the quiet room and shut the door. Once I've done that, I'm 'over the hump' and I'm responding to God's invitation rather than the strident calls of other demands.

The enemy of our souls does not want us to be transformed by God's Word. In the subtleties expressed so well by C S Lewis in *The Screwtape Letters*, even reading long passages of scripture or serving God so there's no time to stop can sometimes be the enemy's shrewd way of distracting us from a depth encounter.

It can be a relief to recognise what's going on. You are not alone if you face inner or outer resistance to getting started. Learn to identify what form your 'hump' takes and walk right over it! A doctor, writing about a stress reduction programme he runs for the chronically ill, says he tells them: 'You don't have to like it. You just have to do it!' This of course is said with compassion and humour. Wholeness, physically or spiritually, doesn't come without commitment. And when we do carry out the commitment, we find we like it after all!

Creating a special place for prayerful meditation is also very helpful in drawing us into the holy place where we meet with God. I'm fortunate to have a room separate from the living area of our house. That may be a luxury few share. A much smaller and simpler place is an old armchair in the corner of my bedroom. On the window sill nearby I have an African stone carving which for me symbolises the Trinity. When I go into my prayer room or sit in the armchair by the window, I feel at once the drawing power of the Spirit beckoning. Places that are prayed in often, develop a prayerful atmosphere.

If you don't already have a 'prayer place', create one. Like my old armchair it can be as simple as a favourite chair in the corner of a room. Try to have a small table, shelf or window sill in front of you where you can place something that reminds you that this is a place to meet God. Your symbols may change from time to time depending on what is significant. Some of the ones I've used are a small pottery cross with a pair of tiny sandals facing it; shells, flowers or other beautiful things from the hand of the Creator; a card with a picture that sums up how I'm feeling; a candle to light as I come to prayer as a sign of welcoming the light of Christ... the possibilities are endless. Once you begin to do this, the symbols themselves will encourage your prayer and you will know when a new one is needed to mark a new phase of your journey.

Other gestures, like taking the phone off the hook, signal to yourself and others that this time has a purpose which takes priority. Whenever I'm tempted to think I don't have time for meditation and prayer, I remember that I always have time to eat three meals a day and to sleep several hours each night. I also have time to watch a bit of TV and read a novel. Time isn't really the problem, however much we may claim that it is!

Best of all, choose a time in the day or the week that you always earmark for meditative prayer. It then becomes part of the habitual rhythm of your life and you are less likely to fight humps of resistance on every occasion.

Choosing scriptures for *Lectio Divina* meditation

Holy reading can be practised with any passage of scripture. It is simply a way of being open to hearing the Word of God at depth, and all of God's words are worthy of such attention. So if you already follow the Lectionary readings in your church tradition, let them be where you begin. Or if you use some other reading plan, approach those readings with the attitude of meditative openness.

Of course, in the nature of this process, you may find you stop on just one verse or thought and do not 'complete' the reading or readings set down for the day. If that feels difficult and gets in the way of being able to 'go slow' and 'stop', then it may be good to devote some particular times to a *Lectio Divina* approach without any competing aims.

You might choose to move meditatively through a book of the Bible that you want to explore. That way you can stop whenever you are drawn to go deeper, knowing that you will simply pick up again at that point next time. Alternatively, you may choose a specific short passage for each time of meditation. At the end of this chapter I will set out some passages on themes that may guide you as you begin.

Sometimes the Holy Spirit brings to mind a well-known scripture or perhaps a fragment half-remembered which seems important to revisit. Take note of such direction and let the process begin at the Spirit's prompting. *Lectio Divina* is an attitude rather than a method. It is a way of receiving God's Word into the deepest parts of our being. While that usually begins with our careful and committed reading, sometimes the Word of God emerges *from* the deepest parts of our being to be welcomed afresh with new meaning.

Journalling the journey

When a gift is unwrapped or a seed begins to sprout, it is good to take note. Writing the outcome of your meditation in a prayer journal records the richness of your encounters with the Living Word. The good thing about writing a journal is that there are no rules! Probably no one but you is ever going to read it. It is a personal and private record of your conversations with God. The children of Israel were often invited to set up altars or stone pillars to mark significant encounters with God so they did not forget his presence on the journey. Jeremiah says: 'Set up road markers for yourself, make yourself guideposts; consider well the highway, the road by which you went' (Jeremiah 31:21).

Journals may contain written prayers, jottings of key insights, a personal psalm or poem, sketches or diagrams, significant scriptures, pictures or cuttings from other sources pasted in because they underline a truth God had been pointing out. Every entry is a 'road marker' on your journey. I find that when I read back in my journal after a few weeks or months, I am freshly amazed at how God has met me and where we have travelled together. I am also amazed at how quickly I forget! That's why the written record is so important. So as you explore meditating on God's Word in the way we have been discussing, keep a record of the soul-reviving treasures that are 'more to be desired ... than gold, even much fine gold' (Psalm 19:10).

✷ Try it

I have chosen seven scripture passages from four areas of scripture: the Psalms, the rest of the Old Testament, the Gospels and the rest of the New Testament. You can select from these scriptures for many weeks of holy reading. Most of the readings are short. This is best for *Lectio Divina* meditation. Where the whole psalm or passage is longer, it may provide several days of meditation. Remember not to feel compelled to 'complete the passage' in one sitting! Remember too that these are simply my choice of some good passages to start with. Any part of the Bible is food for meditation!

You may notice that the Gospel readings are not chosen from the narratives of Jesus interacting with people, but rather are passages of Jesus' teaching. This is because the interactive narratives lend themselves best to another form of meditation, which we will discover in the next chapter!

Psalm 8	How majestic is your name in all the earth!
Psalm 16	Protect me, O God, for in you I take refuge.
Psalm 23	The Lord is my shepherd.
Psalm 37	Do not fret because of the wicked.
Psalm 62	Trust in him at all times, O people.

Psalm 131	I have calmed and quieted my soul.
Psalm 139	O Lord, you have searched me and known me.
Deuteronomy 32:10–12	He sustained him in a desert land.
Joshua 1:5–9	As I was with Moses, so I will be with you.
Song of Solomon 2:8–17	Arise my love, my fair one, and come away.
Isaiah 43:1–7	When you pass through the waters, I will be with you.
Hosea 11:1–9	When Israel was a child, I loved him.
Micah 7:18–20	Who is a God like you, pardoning iniquity..?
Zephaniah 3:14–20	He will rejoice over you with gladness.
Matthew 5:1–12	Blessed are...
Matthew 6:25–34	Do not worry about your life.
Mark 4:21–25	A lamp under a bushel basket.
Luke 6:37,38	Do not judge, and you will not be judged.
John 1:1–18	In the beginning was the Word.
John 14:25–27	Peace I leave with you.
John 15:1–11	Abide in me as I abide in you.
Romans 8:31–39	Who will separate us from the love of Christ?
1 Corinthians 13:1–7	Love is...
Galatians 5:22–26	The fruit of the Spirit.
Ephesians 3:14–21	Strengthened in your inner being.
Philippians 4:10–14	I have learned to be content.
Colossians 2:1–7	God's mystery, that is, Christ himself.
James 1:2–8	If any of you is lacking in wisdom, ask God.

CHAPTER 3
Living the story

It was a life-changing experience. Looking back, I am amazed at how God opened the way for me to do something that might have seemed out of the question. After all, I was a good Protestant woman, born and bred in the Baptist tradition and lecturing at an evangelical Bible college in New Zealand, so why would I want to use my study leave to travel to North Wales and spend three months in a Jesuit spirituality centre training to be a spiritual director?

The year was 1988, and at that time some of my colleagues and employers were shocked at my plan and seriously wondered if I had 'left the fold' of the Protestant evangelical community. I felt a bit shaky myself to be doing such a different and daring thing, and found it hard to explain exactly how I knew this was an invitation from God to move forward in my spiritual journey.

At the heart of the three-month course was a thirty-day Ignatian retreat. I knew from church history that Ignatius of Loyola in sixteenth-century Spain had had a clear conversion experience which had later led him to begin the Jesuit order. Ignatius's vision was for other young men to discover what it really meant to follow Jesus as committed disciples. To enable this to happen, Ignatius devised a way to teach them to meditate and pray their way through the whole of the gospel story, from the birth of Jesus to his ascension. Their text was the Bible. The format for this process developed into a thirty-day retreat, with the whole month set aside for living in the gospel story.

Becoming disciples of Jesus by prayer and meditation on the Gospels sounded pretty evangelical to me! And so it proved to be. In my life to date that month of retreat stands out as the most significant spiritual experience of all. However, I'm glad to tell you that you don't have to set aside a month and go on retreat to experience some of the same riches! The way that Ignatius guided the young men who joined him is a way of living the gospel story that is available to us all. It can be used in a daily time of prayer or on a shorter retreat.

Ignatius wanted to help people *experience* the reality and wonder of Jesus, not just know about it theoretically. As a way to do this, he enouraged the use of our five senses and our imagination.

Coming to our senses

The Creator has generously given us five physical ways to take in and appreciate the swirl of information and impressions that surround us. Take a moment right now to check this out.

- We can **hear** sounds. What do you hear as you tune in? Listen a little more deeply. Is there a far away sound or a quieter one beneath the ones you first heard?

- We can **see** objects, colours, people, shapes, trees, buildings. What's in your immediate field of vision? If you raise your eyes and look around, what else comes into view?

- We can **smell** scents and odours. Is there a pleasant or unpleasant smell you can detect right now? Sniff around a bit if you need to and find at least one!

- We can **taste** our food or anything else we may put in our mouths. You may not be eating right now, but next time you do, give your full attention to the flavour of every mouthful.

- We can **feel** with our sensitive skin, nerves and muscles the texture, shape and temperature of objects we touch or that touch us. Without moving, focus on the feel of your body touching the chair, or the grass you are lying on, or your shoes on your feet. Now reach out and deliberately touch something (or someone) with careful attention to the tactile sensations: rough, smooth, warm, cool, rounded, sharp.

In just those few moments, I hope your appreciation of your five senses was enhanced! All too often we take them for granted. If you have ever had a temporary or permanent disability affecting any of your senses, you will know how valued each one is. All of our senses give us not just information but also delight, appreciation, fun, ways to communicate and sometimes warnings of danger. In addition to the five physical senses, we also 'feel' in an emotional way, and these feelings are often triggered by what we see, hear, smell, taste and touch.

When it comes to entering into the gospel story, our five senses can take us into the full reality of what was happening, at a depth that may surprise you. Ignatius suggests that after a first reading of the particular story, we then go back over it deliberately asking: 'If I were there, what would I hear? What would I see? What would I smell? What would I taste? What would I feel?'

Take, for example, the narrative of the birth of Jesus: 'Joseph also went from the town of Nazareth in Galilee to Judea, to the city of David called Bethlehem, because he was descended from the house and family of David. He went to be registered with Mary, to whom he was engaged and who was expecting a child. While they were there, the time came for her to deliver her child. And she gave birth to her firstborn son and wrapped him in bands of cloth, and laid him in a manger, because there was no place for them in the inn.' (Luke 2:4–7)

To 'be there' with your five senses opens up a kaleidoscope of impressions: the dust and noise of animals and people travelling together; the cold air and bundles of clothes pulled tight; aching muscles on the ninety-mile walk; the bumpy spine of the donkey under Mary; her heavy body weary with nine months of pregnancy; the smell of sweat and animal dung; the welcome taste of food and wine at a rest stop; the early darkness falling and the emerging stars giving light. And then the labour pains beginning; the voices of innkeepers saying, 'Sorry, no room'; the feel of Joseph's arm round Mary's shoulders; the welcome warmth of animal bodies and the sight of their breath in the cave's shadows. Later the groans of a woman in labour and her laughing tears as a baby is born. Now there are the welcome cries of the little one and the business-like conversation of those who helped with the delivery. We hear Joseph's sigh of relief and notice Mary welcoming even the straw to lie back on and rest. Soon there are the snuffling, snuggling sounds of Jesus at Mary's breast and his secure feeling at being swaddled and placed carefully in the manger.

And that's just a sample! I'm sure as you enter the story and notice what your five senses suggest, there are many more possibilities. Most of the time it's not necessary to go through the five senses one by one as if by rote. It's more a decision to take a sensate look at the story and let all the senses combine as they draw you in.

Sometimes, though, if you find it hard to get started, it can help to ask quite deliberately what you would see, hear, smell, taste or touch. Some people can enter a scene easily and vividly, almost 'hearing and seeing' it all happen on the screen of their mind. Others come to a heightened awareness of the scene more intangibly with a kind of 'inner sense or knowing' of what it might have been like. Either way is fine! I've sometimes led groups of people in this way of meditating on a Gospel story and had those who weren't 'vividly visual' feel as if they hadn't done it right. Not so! I'm not vividly visual myself but I know that by choosing to bring my senses to the story, I enter it with a depth of reality that wasn't there before.

Of course, entering a story via the senses puts us in touch with the emotions and challenges of the story as well. We, like the people in the actual events, are whole people. Physical, emotional, mental and spiritual responses intertwine and cannot be easily separated. So, as we set the scene with our senses, we identify emotionally with one or more of the people present. You may empathise with Mary through the anxiety of wondering if she'd reach a private birthing place in time. You may be right there with Joseph feeling responsible for Mary and angry at the innkeepers. You might find yourself standing in awe in a corner of the cave, watching it all happen with tears of wonder flowing.

Entering the story may give rise to some new questions: What did Mary think about all this? Hadn't she been told this was a very special baby? Did she doubt? Did she think, 'This is a pretty poor deal, God!'? Or did her trust give her a peace and confidence that others would not have understood? What about Joseph – did he start to wish he had broken off this engagement? Did he think he'd got it all wrong and God couldn't possibly be in all this? Of course we can't know, but realising that these were real, flesh and blood people like us brings home the reality with which they had to grapple.

Even if we can't know what Mary and Joseph thought and felt, entering the story will highlight what we ourselves think and feel. If you had been Mary, or Joseph, how would you be reacting? Even if you'd been an observer back then, would you have had any clue that

God was behind this whole event? What would you have felt about it? Of course, you are an observer right now. How is the story affecting you? What feelings arise? What are you learning? What questions are you asking? What do you want to discuss with God about it all? Ignatius says that as we enter a story in this way, our aim is to 'draw much fruit' from the experience.

It is helpful to record the most important fruit of a prayerful entering into the gospel. Here's what I wrote after my own meditation on this passage:

'Lord, as I put myself in the story of Mary and Joseph, I am reminded again of how strange your ways are sometimes. Everything seems to be going wrong and I can't work out why you don't do something. Yet in this story everything was really going according to plan – your plan. Help me to trust you, God, when you seem to take me away from my familiar places and supportive people just when I think I need them most. And when the door of the inn shuts in my face when I specially prayed you would open it, then help me to expect to find a different place in my experience for you to be born.'

Where does imagination fit in?

I wonder if we realise how vital imagination is to human life. Like the five senses, it is a God-given gift to enable us to live life fully and deeply. Imagination allows us to move beyond the confines of the present moment and beyond a purely self-centred view of the world. I recently watched a series of programmes on child development. It was fascinating to realise that before a child develops the capacity to imagine, she can only comprehend what is actually happening right now. As soon as that person or toy or event is gone, it simply does not exist for the child. There is no imaginative capacity to hold the image or the feeling and know it is real, even if it is not here right now.

Without imagination, you could not have entered into the story of the birth of Jesus and let it come alive for you now. Without imagination, you cannot empathise with another person because you would not have the capacity to see things from their point of view. Without imagination, you could not recall the wonderful holiday you had last year nor plan what you would like to do next holiday! We use imagination constantly both to remember and to plan. We use it to relate sensitively to others and to prepare for the likely consequences of our actions. We use it when we relax with a good book or movie. We value the way it enables us to recall the faces of absent family members or friends. In short, we can't do without it!

The Jewish people use imagination at every Passover meal to recall and relive the events of the journey out of Egypt. In fact, all the Jewish feast days and celebrations are a deliberate way of keeping alive faith in God's goodness by remembering vividly now what had happened long ago.

Jesus called on people's imagination all the time. He was constantly telling stories and painting word pictures. He asked people to imagine the kingdom of God as a mustard seed, as yeast, as a treasure hidden in a field. He asked them to imagine themselves as soil for seeds to land on, or to take an imaginative leap from the birds of the air and the lilies of the field to their own ability to trust. He described himself as a mother hen and as a person noticing a fallen sparrow and wanted those images to convey his loving care for us. Jesus also transformed the Passover meal, giving it a new meaning to be remembered. Every time we take the bread and wine at a communion service, we use our imagination to enter the reality of Jesus' body broken and blood poured out for us.

It is against this background that we can place the questions and hesitations that some have about imagination. Although we use our imaginative capacity all the time without even realising it, when it comes to using imagination deliberately as a way of meditating on biblical passages, some people recoil in dismay. Surely if it is 'all in the imagination', that means it is not true, that it's made up or fanciful, doesn't it? Of course it is true that we can use our imagination to make up stories and scenes that are fanciful and not related to actual events. That's how novels are written and wonderful children's stories created. But using our imagination to enter more fully into a story that did actually happen is altogether different. Imagination, like any other human capacity, can be used under the guidance of the Holy Spirit. Since it is a gift of God, God is surely delighted when we use it prayerfully to bring us into a deeper relationship with him.

Living, as many of us do, in a Western, rationalistic culture, we tend to trust our cognitive and intellectual processes more than the imaginative, symbolic ways of knowing. Yet, if you stop to think about it, our thoughts and reasoning can just as easily be off-centre, leading us away from truth and from God. All our human capacities are flawed and need to be brought to the light of God's Spirit. Similarly, all of our human capacities are wonderful treasures to be valued and used wisely to bring us to fullness of life.

With that in mind, let's go one step further into this way of living the gospel story. Ignatius began every meditation with a prayer that the grace of God would flow through every part of his meditation so that his whole being would be directed more fully to the praise and service of God. What a wonderful way to begin! Now we can enter the gospel story with anticipation that through it we will be guided by God's grace to whatever it is we most need to take us forward in our own story.

His story, their story, my story

One of the wonderful things that happens when meditating in this way is that the historical story merges into our contemporary story. Jesus is the same yesterday, today and for ever. The person who interacted with men, women and children in Israel two thousand years ago is alive still and wants to interact with us. His compassion and love and power and challenging questions are there for us just as much as for the people he met long ago.

What this means, of course, is that at some point in living the historical story you will find your own current story coming into focus in the light of the gospel. The story on the page enlightens and challenges the story you are living. Let me give you a personal example.

The story of Peter walking on the water has always fascinated me.

One day as I entered into it with my five senses and my imagination, I lived through the story up to the point where Jesus invites Peter to trust him and step out of the boat. I found myself wanting to identify with Peter and live the rest of the story through his eyes. But I couldn't! I just couldn't bring myself, even in imagination, to step out into that raging lake and believe I wouldn't drown. So I stayed in the boat, huddled in a back corner, disappointed in myself and just watching what happened. I vicariously went through the delight and then dismay that Peter felt as he walked and then sank. I watched with bated breath as Jesus caught him by the hand and brought him safely back to the boat. I gasped with absolute amazement when it suddenly went quiet and the storm abated. Like the other disciples, I was overcome with awe and worship. But along with the awe and worship I had a deep sense of sadness and a longing that I had been the one to step out in trust. What a lot I'd missed by being so cautious and fearful.

As you can see, the gospel story had become my story. But because it was my story, something different happened. I was not Peter. I was Sheila, not ready at that point to do what Peter did. Finding that out was very important to what was going on in my life at that time. I stayed with what I had discovered and talked to Jesus about it. What happened in that conversation was humbling and powerful. While I was still in the meditation, sitting in the back corner of the boat feeling sad at what I'd missed, Jesus noticed me and came to me. That was the first surprise! I would have thought he had eyes only for Peter. He compassionately let me know he understood my longing and my not being ready yet. That was the second surprise. There was no rebuke or judgement about my level of trust. There was an invitation, though. It was as if he gently pointed out that there would be other times to walk on water in the storm and maybe next time I would be ready!

That meditation took place some years ago and looking back now I can see that I have been able to step out of my secure boat into some pretty risky waters. I believe the Spirit of God was at work in that meditation to show me something I needed to see and to enable me to move forward in the days ahead by the grace of God.

Letting the story become your story and listening to how Jesus may personally meet you is one of the ways we 'gain much fruit' from the meditation. Entering the story imaginatively and noticing what we feel, or who we identify with, or what we do or say, is a powerful way for the Holy Spirit to reveal to us things we may not have seen so clearly before. It means, too, that you can return to the same story another time and discover that you are in a different place. The gospel is living not static! Jesus always meets us where we actually are now, not where we were last time or where we wished we were.

The ways you personally connect with a Gospel story can vary. Sometimes there is an immediate identification with one character in the story. You know you are like them in some way and live the story through their eyes. Other times you may find you are an observer in the crowd, just watching it all and being aware of your own response. It really doesn't matter how it happens. Having prayed that the Spirit of God would guide your meditation, trust that he will.

Putting it all together

Having explored what Ignatius had in mind in developing this way of living the gospel story, let's review the steps.

1 Pray that God's grace will guide your meditation. Ask him to use your mind, your senses, your imagination to direct you towards worship, insight and growth.

2 Read a Gospel passage. Choose a segment that has a complete story, especially one where Jesus is interacting with people.

3 Having read the passage, enter into it again as if you were there, letting your senses and your imagination open it up in depth. This is the heart of the meditation, so take as long as you need for this. If the story begins to become your story, let that happen. Cooperate with the Spirit and notice what is brought to light.

4 Take some time to reflect on what happened in your meditation. Record the fruit of the experience in your journal.

Getting started

It's often helpful to have someone lead you in an Ignatian meditation the first few times, just to get started. Since I can't come
alongside and do that in person, I'm including some written examples that might give you some prompts along the way. Once you
begin to experience the power of living the story, you won't need my
suggestions any more! You'll be able to let any part of the gospel
story become your story.

Feeding the five thousand

Take a moment to settle in a relaxed and quiet place. Make sure you
have your Bible and a pen and journal with you. Pray for God's grace
and the Spirit's guidance as you enter this story.

Read Mark 6:30–44.

*(As you proceed through the meditation, pause every time you see an ellipsis or
paragraph break, and notice your own feelings, thoughts and responses.)*

Now join the disciples. It has been a busy time for you recently, so
much happening in work and ministry, exciting but tiring, sometimes not even enough time to eat ... Jesus is suggesting a day away
together for some quietness and rest. What is your response to that
idea? ... What are you hoping for?

The boat is launched and the trip across the lake in a light breeze
is pleasant ... Feel the motion of the boat on the water ... let the sun
warm you ... What is the mood among the disciples? ... What are you
doing? ... Let all your senses take in the atmosphere.

As you arrive at the remote destination on the far side of the lake,
you notice crowds of people have got there before you ... What is
your reaction to that? ... What are the other disciples saying? ...
What is the mood among you now?... Look at Jesus and notice how
he is responding.

Jesus spends a long time teaching the people who have gathered.
Take in the scene with all your senses. See the crowd sitting on the
grass or standing round the edges of the group straining to hear ...

Look at Jesus ... What do you notice about him? ... Listen to Jesus' voice compassionately ringing out ... Notice other sounds: the lapping of the lake, the laughter of playful children ... What else do you hear? ... What smells waft in the air? ... How does your body feel? ... What emotions jostle for attention as the hours go by? ... Are you with other disciples? ... What goes on among you?

The day is coming to an end. It has not been what you expected at all ... How are you feeling at this end of the day? ... Some of your friends suggest that Jesus should send the people away to get food ... You listen eagerly for his response ... He says: 'You give them something to eat!' What is your reaction as you hear this? ... Do you say out loud what you are thinking? ... Why or why not?

You stand with the other disciples as the meagre fare of five loaves and two fish are brought forward. Look at them ... notice the smell of bread and fish at the end of a long hungry day ... What's going on inside you?

Now Jesus is telling you to get all the people seated in orderly groups ... There are thousands of them! ... What is your attitude as you walk among the crowd organising them into manageable clusters? ... Look at them all ... men, women, children ... tired after a long day, but excited at what Jesus has been saying ... Listen to snatches of their conversation as you move around ... Feel the change in temperature as the day turns to evening.

When you come back to where Jesus is, you see that he's raising the bread and fish and giving thanks to God ... What goes through your mind as you watch? ... Then he hands each of you some broken pieces to give out ... It takes ages ... you have to keep coming back for more ... and there always is more ... What's happening for you as you keep moving to and fro and seeing everyone get enough? ... What do you see and hear among the gathered people as they realise they will all be fed?

Finally, everyone has had enough and Jesus tells you to go and gather up what's left over ... You walk thoughtfully through the satisfied crowd letting them put in your basket what has not been eaten ... Before long there's a whole picnic basket full of food for you.

You sit down a little way from the edge of the crowd and eat ... This food is special food ... taste every mouthful ... Jesus is close by. Do you want to talk with him? ... Whether you talk or not, just sit there for a while taking in what's happened and what it might all mean for you.

When you are ready, take some time to write down how living in this story relates to your story. What has come into clearer focus about Jesus or about yourself? Maybe there are still some unanswered questions. Note them, too, so you can revisit them at some other time. Give thanks for the fruit of this meditation!

Who touched me?

In this meditation, I invite you to identify with the woman who is the key character. Let her experience show you afresh how Jesus meets needy people.

Settle quietly with a Bible and journal at hand. Breathe deeply and slowly as you relax and open yourself to God's Word and the Spirit's guidance.

Read Luke 8:40–48.

The crowd is thick, bodies press together, the dust is stirred up by many sandalled feet, eager voices discuss what Jesus might do this time ... How do you feel as you try to merge unobtrusively with the crowd? ... You know that if anyone knew of your problem, you would be ostracised, avoided and probably punished for being here. What makes you take the risk? ... Tune in to what's happening in your body ... in your emotions ... in your mind.

What is your strategy for getting through the crowd towards Jesus? ... As you edge closer and closer, you hear that important religious man, Jairus, begging Jesus to come quickly to see his daughter ... What goes through your mind? ... What do you expect to happen next? ... What happens to your hopes and your plans for your encounter with Jesus?

The pace of the crowd picks up as everyone moves with Jesus towards Jairus's house ... You are swept along with them ... It is now or never ... Feel yourself reaching out to at least touch the back of his garment ... What goes through your mind as you do?

And now! Register in your body what has happened! ... What mix of emotions well up as you realise you are healed? ... What do you most want to do right now?

Before you can take it all in, you hear Jesus say, 'Who touched me?' ... How do you feel as you realise he knows someone touched him in a special way? ... Are you eager or hesitant to let him know it was you?

What is it like to see the crowd stop and look for the person who will answer Jesus' question? ... What is it like to see Jesus looking around with interest for the person whose whole story he wants to hear?

As you identify yourself and tell your story, what goes on inside you? ... What do you most want Jesus to know about you? ... Are you looking at him to gauge his reaction? ... Notice the posture and body language of both you and Jesus as you are there together in the midst of curious onlookers.

Listen carefully to the words Jesus says to you: 'Daughter...' What does it mean to you to be called 'daughter'? ... 'Your faith has healed you' ... Reflect on the fact that Jesus sees the faith that brought you to this point ... 'Go in peace!' ... Peace ... Peace ... What a beautiful gift ... How will you live it out now? ... What difference will this encounter with Jesus make to the rest of your life? ... Find your own way to say goodbye to Jesus for now ... Do you go on with the crowd to Jairus's house or slip away somewhere quiet to process all that has happened?

Take time now to gather the fruit of this experience. What does this Gospel passage tell you about Jesus? Where did you most strongly identify? How does it relate to your own story? Your particular need will not be identical to the woman in this story, but what do you want as you reach out to touch Jesus? What are his words to *you* as you tell him *your* story?

Mary and Martha

In this meditation, I invite you to do something a bit different: to see the story through both Martha and Mary's eyes. You may naturally identify more with one than the other, but probably there are elements of both characters within each of us. See what happens!

Find a quiet place with enough time to feel unhurried. Have your Bible and journal handy. Notice how you feel as you anticipate entering this Gospel story. Offer your feelings to God and open yourself to his loving direction.

Read Luke 10:38–42.

First let your imagination give you a picture of Mary and Martha's home. It was probably a simple village home but big enough for the sisters and their brother Lazarus to live together. How do you picture the room where Jesus was invited to visit? ... Where did Martha prepare the food? ... It was an inviting place where Jesus felt welcome.

We read that 'Martha opened her home to him'. Let yourself enter Martha's world ... As Martha, what is important to you? ... What do you do to make Jesus welcome? ... How do you feel about him coming today? ... What are you doing by way of preparation? ... How are you feeling? ... What are you thinking and saying to yourself?

You glance over to where Jesus is sitting and see Mary relaxed at his feet ... What happens when you see that? ... Go over to Jesus and say what you are thinking! ... Listen carefully to his response ... Hear the tone of his voice as he understands exactly how it is for you ... What is your response? ... How will you process what Jesus is saying? ... Take time to notice what you do next ... What you say ... What you feel.

When you are ready (and don't hurry), step out of Martha's role and experience this story from Mary's point of view.

You know Martha has invited Jesus to visit. How is this for you? ... What do you feel? ... What do you hope for? ... You see him coming ... How do you welcome him? ... When he is comfortably settled, what do you do? ... As you sit at Jesus' feet listening, what do you imagine he might be talking about? ... Do you enter into a conversation with him or just listen? ... Are you aware of where Martha is and what she's doing? ... If you are, what do you think about it? ... What is it like for you being here while she works?

When Martha comes over and speaks crossly to Jesus about you, how do you feel? ... Before you can respond you hear his reply ... Now what happens for you? ... Notice how you respond to what Jesus has said .... Take note too of how you are with Martha ... Is there anything the two of you need to talk about?

Take some time now to 'draw much fruit' from this experience. What did you discover about who you most easily identified with? Are the gifts of Martha and Mary well balanced in you? What might Jesus be wanting to draw to your attention from this Gospel event?

Keep on living the story!

Now you can choose your own Gospel stories and live your way into them! You could choose one of the Gospels and move through it chronologically, using this way of meditating on Jesus' interactions with people. Mark or Luke might be the best place to start. Or you might browse through the Gospels, looking at the headings of different incidents and choosing one that seems to invite you in. You may well find that at particular times the Spirit will bring a story to mind. If that happens, take notice! Remember that one of the Spirit's specific roles is to 'remind you of everything I [Jesus] have said to you' (John 14:26).

So keep on living the story and let it become your story...

CHAPTER 4
Meditation on the move

Have you ever thought about how much of what we know about prayer from biblical examples took place outside, on the move, in the natural environment of creation? Prayer wasn't confined to the synagogue or temple, or even to one's room with a closed door. Of course all of those places were good places for prayer at appropriate times, but that's only half the story!

- I'm sure Abraham prayed as he climbed the mountain, thinking he was asked to sacrifice Isaac (Genesis 22).

- Later Isaac's servant stood by a village well and prayed for God's guidance in choosing his master a wife (Genesis 24:10–14).

- Isaac himself was out in the field meditating, when his servant returned with Rebekah (Genesis 24:63).

- Moses had powerful prayer experiences before a burning bush (Exodus 3), on the brink of the Red Sea (Exodus 14:13–18) and in many desert journey crises (eg Exodus 15:22–27; 17:1–7).

- Miriam led the Israelites in a vibrant prayerful song and dance after crossing the Red Sea (Exodus 15:1–21).

- Joshua and the priests carrying the ark of the Covenant enacted their prayerful trust in God by stepping into the river Jordan (Joshua 3).

- The capture of Jericho was achieved after a symbolic seven-day walk where no words were spoken and which culminated in a shout of victory (Joshua 6).

- David sang many of his prayerful psalms while out caring for the sheep (eg Psalm 8, 23).

- Jeremiah was spoken to by God as he stood watching a potter at work (Jeremiah 18).

- Jesus went up a mountain to pray before choosing the disciples (Mark 6:46).

- An unnamed woman told Jesus her whole tragic story in the middle of a crowd of jostling people (Luke 8:40–48).

- Jesus took his close friends up a mountain for the powerful experience of his transfiguration (Luke 9:28).
- Jesus' agonised prayer before his death took place in a garden (Matthew 26:36–46).
- One of Peter's most significant talks with Jesus happened after a lakeside breakfast (John 21:15–22).

These examples invite us to step into a new arena for prayer: prayer on the move, prayer in the context of everyday experience, prayer stimulated by creation. Meditating on what God wants to say to us is not confined to words on a page, sacred and wonderful as such words may be. The living Word of God comes to us in many ways. One of the Holy Spirit's roles is to teach us, remind us, interpret for us the truth here and now in our own experience (John 14:25,26; 15:26). In this chapter we'll explore meditation particularly on, and in, creation. We'll save some other aspects of prayer in the often busy rush of life's experiences for a chapter of its own!

Let me share with you a personal experience of prayer on the move and in creation.

Wild, winter worship

On my way home from work one winter afternoon, I suddenly felt the urge to drive out of the city to a wild ocean beach. It seemed rather an odd thing to do. There was a strong, cold wind and only an hour before darkness – not the best beach-walking conditions! But I followed the inner nudge and drove on.

As I drove, I reflected on how powerfully I feel connected to God when I am close to his creation. 'The heavens are telling the glory of God; and the firmament proclaims his handiwork. Day to day pours forth speech, and night to night declares knowledge' (Psalm 19:1,2). Of course, my spirit and God's Spirit have a chance to meet when I am close to the work of his hands.

'Well, Lord,' I thought as I pulled up at the beach, 'it's a grey, freezing day and most people would think I'm crazy coming out here. But you and I are here together, so what do you have to show me?'

Down on the beach I discovered that a winter gale on a New Zealand, west coast beach is like a snowstorm. Great balls of foam race across the sand, icing mounds of seaweed and piling up against the steps for all the world like a snowdrift. Bigger foam piles shiver in the freezing wind and then break up and skim like ice skaters across the steely grey sand.

I am like a child in my delight as I watch and kick and run to catch a foam ball. The skaters are far too fast for me. They whisk around my feet playfully, caressing my shoes with a touch so light it cannot be felt. I laugh at myself as I grab and miss. I can almost hear the ocean laughing with me. There is a tangible connection of energy, delight and joy between the elements and me. I feel it blowing into me and around me as I stand facing the wind and exult in the roar of the ocean. In this present moment there is nothing between me and the power of the Creator pounding in the ocean, dancing in the skating foam balls and surging in the wind that nearly blows me off my feet.

A primitive joy that has nothing to do with the circumstances of my life rises from my belly and surges like the surf through all the crevices of my being, demanding expression in a shout of delight.

Bundled in a parka, woolly hat, scarf and gloves, I am dressed for worship. Standing alone, laughing into the wind, I join all creation in praise. Marvelling that the cliff top plants are not blown out by the roots is sermon enough: how deep are my roots? What storms must they withstand?

The Spirit led me out to the wilds of Muriwai beach that day I am sure. It wasn't a 'sensible' thing to do on such a day but the urge was insistent. 'Continue to be insistent in me, Creative God. Break me out of my sensible, anxious, boring boundaries and fill me again and again with the wind and dancing foam of your Spirit.'

Knowing the Creator

'For what can be known about God is plain to them, because God has shown it to them. Ever since the creation of the world his eternal power *and divine nature, invisible though they are, have been understood and seen through the things he has made. So they are without excuse'* (Romans 1:19,20).

This verse should alert us to the importance of valuing one of the ways God wants to make himself known. As the Celtic saint Columbanus put it: 'If you want to know the Creator, understand created things.' It makes sense, doesn't it? Any creative work tells you a great deal about the creator. A painter paints what he or she wants to show you of their perspective on life. A craftsman's work tells you immediately a lot about his skill, his care, what he values. Even a home-cooked meal reveals the cook's taste, culinary skill and maybe even her mood! In fact, it is actually impossible to create anything *without* revealing something of yourself. You, after all, are the one who decides what to create, chooses the media and carries out the process. How could it *not* reveal some clues about your character, your gifts, your values?

God is the supreme Creator. The Bible opens with the moving poetic account of God as Creator of the heavens and the earth out of a formless void of darkness. We wouldn't even be here in our marvellous world but for the creativity of God. Every detail of the smallest flower and the most enormous animal was God's idea. A creative God decided every snowflake would have an individual design and every human fingerprint would be unique. The Creator of this world gave every plant and animal a special place in the interdependent community of living things. God loves a profusion of colour and variety. God cares about the tiniest insect or butterfly having beautiful markings. And as for the whole universe beyond our tiny planet earth... well, as the psalmist David said, 'When I look at your heavens, the work of your fingers, the moon and the stars that you have established; what are human beings that you are mindful of them, mortals that you care for them? ... O Lord, our Sovereign, how majestic is your name in all the earth!' (Psalm 8:3,4,9)

I spend quite a lot of my time talking with people about their relationship with God, eg those I introduced in chapter 1. Often, if they are struggling to pray or feeling they aren't getting anything out of the Bible, I ask: 'When *do* you feel most in touch with God?' Nine times out of ten the answer is: 'When I'm out in creation'. The wording of their answers varies – it might be 'When I'm out walking', 'In the garden', 'Out on a deserted beach' or 'Tramping in the hills'. However it is worded, God's creation is a place where many people are most naturally put in touch with the Creator, and that's exactly as it should be. The funny thing is that when I encourage people to use what they've just told me as one of their most helpful ways of praying, they often look surprised, shocked or downright sceptical! 'But walking on the beach can't be praying, can it?' (Isn't that too easy?) 'You mean, I can experience *gardening* as a kind of meditation?' (Isn't that cheating somehow?) 'Isn't this business of finding God in creation really pantheism or something?' (Careful, this could be heresy!) I understand their concerns. After all, most of us have been taught that prayer is about words, that meditation must certainly be meditation on a passage of scripture and that most of it is done with your eyes closed. So we need some time to adjust our perspective. But if the scriptures themselves encourage us to see 'God's eternal power and divine nature ... through the things he has made', then who are we to hesitate?

Of course, it's quite possible to walk and garden and be immersed in creation without it being prayerful or meditative in the least. Perhaps, sadly, that's the norm. We take creation for granted most of the time, and cease to be in awe and wonder before the Creator. It's also possible to see creation as somehow containing God and being God. That's pantheism's mistake but probably not one we would genuinely fall into. It is as foolish as deciding that all of Monet's paintings put together actually contain, define and are the being of Claude Monet, that there is no person beyond the paintings. It doesn't make sense, does it? No, our problem is not giving creation too much value, but hardly seeing the Creator's message at all. The eyes of our heart, as well as our physical eyes, need to be open to respond.

✷ **Try it**

Take some time to be outside, in the garden or walking somewhere you enjoy. Ask God to be your companion and to show you something of his 'eternal power and divine nature'. As you walk or sit or garden, simply be alert to what God wants you to see. Your attention may be drawn to God's love for colour and beauty, or attention to detail, or amazing design skills, or care in providing what is needed for life and growth... or something else!

When you have noticed what qualities of the Creator are demonstrated, think about how those same qualities impact on you as part of God's creation. For example, if you are struck by how God equips living things to adapt to their environment, think about how God helps you to adapt to what you face in your own life.

From blindness to sight

I recently heard a phrase that caught my attention: 'We are dead to everything we take for granted.' I'd like to rephrase it as: 'We are blind to everything we take for granted.' One of the stories that powerfully illustrates *not* taking things for granted is the story of Sheila Hocken, told in her book *Emma and I*.

In 1946 Sheila was born to two visually-impaired parents. For the first few years of her life, she could see a little – through a blurry indistinct haze. But by the time she started school, Sheila was blind.

The story of her life – including her life with her beloved guide dog Emma – is a fascinating insight into a world without sight. But the part of her story I want to quote comes thirty years later when advances in eye surgery made possible an operation that restored Sheila's sight.

The day the bandages came off for the first time she says:

'What happened then – the only way I can describe the sensation – is that I was suddenly hit, physically struck by brilliance, like an immense electric shock into my brain and through my entire body. It flooded my whole being with a shock-wave, this utterly unimaginable, incandescent brightness: there was white in front of me, a dazzling white that I could hardly bear to take in, and a vivid blue that I had never thought possible. It was fantastic, marvellous, incredible. It was like the beginning of the world.'

The white and blue were the colours of the nurses' uniforms!

Each day for several days, Sheila could only have the bandages removed for a few minutes:

'Every morning when the moment arrived for the bandages to be removed I had a flicker of doubt: "Will it be as bright again, will it be as beautiful?" Each day it was and the anxieties faded from my mind. Each day I chose something I would look at in my few moments of sight. One day I took a bunch of dahlias someone had brought for me. I had never liked dahlias because they had no scent but when the bandages were removed I looked down at my dahlias and saw that they were a gorgeous yellow that I had never imagined, and that they seemed so intricately made. I was fascinated by their every detail, and so remorseful that I had not appreciated them before...'

The time came for Sheila to leave the hospital, and for the first time she walked outside as a sighted person:

'The sunshine burst in on me and once more it was as I had imagined the birth of the world. Of course I knew that it had been like this for millions and millions of years, or so my rational mind told me, but I still felt it was the entire creation, suddenly laid on for my personal benefit. I was seeing for the first time something which everyone else was used to and took for granted, and its impression on me was unique.

'Beyond the sunshine and immediate glaring radiance I saw a great expanse of green.

' "What's that?"

' "Why it's grass of course."

'Grass? Of course. It had to be. Something I had felt through the soles of my shoes. "But it is so green. I can't believe it. Is it always like this?" Don said it was, but I had to kneel down and touch it to make sure it was what I had felt before.

' "But it's all different shades, all different greens. Even the separate blades seem to differ in colour."

' "Yes, it's always like that."

' "It's so marvellous, so beautiful."'

Maybe it would do us all good to be blind for a while so that we might learn to see again! Certainly we can ask God to heal our spiritual blindness and cause us to see the creative character of our God spread out prolifically before our eyes.

✴ Try it

Choose some aspect of creation that interests or attracts you. It may be small enough to hold in your hand, like a flower or a shell or an insect; or it may be as big as the tree outside your window or as vast as the ocean rolling in front of you.

Examine whatever you have chosen as if you are seeing it for the first time. Use as many of your senses as you can: touch it, smell it, listen for any associated sounds, perhaps taste it too, and certainly look intently at every detail. Take time to do this in a relaxed and enquiring way. Don't assume anything. Try to see this part of creation as if you have never seen it before. Ask the Creator to 'show you round' this particular piece of his handiwork, pointing out things you might otherwise miss or take for granted.

Respond in some way to what you have seen. You might want to write your own psalm. You might want to draw or paint what you have now seen with fresh eyes. You may simply want to give thanks!

God's delight, our delight

Have you ever thought what fun God might have had creating such a varied, amazing world? I don't mean to trivialise the majesty of God or the intricate artistry of creation by suggesting there was fun involved, but really – the elephant's trunk, the pelican's beak, the kangaroo's pouch, the fly-catching plants, the colourful coral... Surely we can catch some of God's delight and enjoyment in bringing it all into being?

When we take delight in what God delights to create, we join him in celebration. And that's no small thing. To join our heart's delight with God's by appreciating what he has made, brings us into relationship. To be in awe at the wonder of a butterfly emerging from a dark chrysalis is to meditate reverently on God's handiwork. To have no words but 'Oooooh!' as we watch a sunset is to express praise. To walk a woodland path enjoying the dappled patterns of sunlight and shadow and breathing in the scent of pine needles and honeysuckle is to wordlessly express thanksgiving to the Creator.

I believe that our delight in creation brings delight to God's heart. God's creative delight is met by our appreciative response and God is delighted. A circle is completed.

Although we are using the word 'meditation' as a theme in this book, perhaps the word 'contemplation' will also add to our understanding of this way of praying. 'Contemplation' comes from the root word 'templum', which originally meant a special place set aside for the observation of creation and being in touch with the awe and mystery of the Creator. Long before the Christian era people set aside such places (usually outdoors) for the purpose of becoming more aware of the divine.

Biblically we are very familiar with the word 'temple' (which of course comes from the same root) and all that it means in terms of worship of God. The temple was always the place where one paid special, focused attention to God. That can be done just as well in the 'templum' of creation as in a building. The word 'contemplate' has come across into secular terminology to mean paying special, focused attention to anything. The *Oxford English Dictionary* says to contemplate is 'to look at with continued attention, gaze upon, ponder, observe'. As Christians we can reclaim the essentially God-focused dimension of the word and see contemplation as a way of prayerfully paying attention to God's character shown in creation.

When we contemplate creation, we pay attention to what is really there – a tree, a flower, a landscape – but we also learn to see behind or beyond what is there to the greater spiritual reality. For example, I can look at a tree and see 'just the same old tree', or I can pause to contemplate the tree and see the wonder of its construction, its beauty, its withstanding of the wind… and be drawn to worship the Creator who designed it all.

✸ Try it

Go for a contemplative walk. When I walk contemplatively, I walk much more slowly than usual so that I can reverently gaze at what is before me. Stop when something in God's creation invites you to observe more deeply and ponder. Take delight in God's handiwork and let your appreciation be your worship.

A contemplative walk is a lovely thing to do with others. Don't talk to each other as you walk, but after the walk is over, compare notes about what you noticed and give thanks together.

Gaining perspective

I once heard a renowned theologian give an illustration which has never left me. He said: 'Come with me to the beach. Pick up a handful of sand. Let it run through your fingers until a single grain remains. Let that single grain represent our planet earth. Then look to the right and the left at all the grains of sand on the beach and realise that they are equivalent to the other planets and stars in our galaxy.

'Then pick up another handful of sand … let one grain now represent our galaxy. Now the other grains of sand represent the other galaxies in the known universe.'

Surely it is evident that 'the heavens are telling the glory of God; and the firmament proclaims his handiwork' (Psalm 19:1)?

Whether it is the incomprehensible vastness of the universe or the breathtaking detail on the wing of a tiny moth, creation has a way of putting things back in perspective. Seeing the world from an egocentric point of view (which we all quite naturally do) does not help us to grasp reality from a God-centric point of view. Of course, in this life we will never completely share God's perspective, but to shift our centre of vision even for a moment opens up possibilities for hope and faith.

C S Lewis said that creation did not teach him the word 'glory' but it gave it meaning for him. The psalmist seems to have had the same experience: 'Ascribe to the Lord the glory of his name; worship the Lord in holy splendour. The voice of the Lord is over the waters; the God of glory thunders, the Lord, over mighty waters ... The voice of the Lord flashes forth flames of fire. The voice of the Lord shakes the wilderness; the Lord shakes the wilderness of Kadesh. The voice of the Lord causes the oaks to whirl, and strips the forest bare; and in his temple all say, "Glory!"' (Psalm 29:2–4,7–9).

Many events in our lives and in the global village in which we live cannot be answered or explained in words or by reason. There are many things we will never understand with human logic. The story of Job illustrates the point. After all the human misery and suffering Job had been through, God's answer to Job was an almost overwhelming litany of the marvels of creation as if to say: 'Look, listen – here I am. You feel deserted but I am surrounding you with powerful evidence of my presence in everything you observe.'

Here are the first and last paragraphs of God's first speech to Job. I hope you'll read all that lies between!

' *"Where were you when I laid the foundation of the earth? Tell me, if you have understanding. Who determined its measurements – surely you know! Or who stretched the line upon it? On what were its bases sunk, or who laid its cornerstone when the morning stars sang together and all the heavenly beings shouted for joy? Or who shut in the sea with doors when it burst out from the womb? – when I made the clouds its garment, and thick darkness its swaddling band, and prescribed bounds for it, and set bars and doors, and said, 'Thus far shall you come, and no farther, and here shall your proud waves be stopped'?" ' (Job 38:4–11)*

' "Is it by your wisdom that the hawk soars, and spreads its wings toward the south? Is it at your command that the eagle mounts up and makes its nest on high? It lives on the rock and makes its home in the fastness of the rocky crag. From there it spies the prey; its eyes see it from far away. Its young ones suck up blood; and where the slain are, there it is." '
(Job 39:26–30)

And after hearing all that Job says: 'I know that you can do all things, and that no purpose of yours can be thwarted ... I had heard of you by the hearing of the ear, but now my eye sees you' (Job 42:2,5).

To some of life's experiences there are no 'answers' that can satisfy our logic. But to place ourselves in the context of God's mighty works can bring a peace and a humility born of a new perspective.

✷ Try it

When you are in a situation that seems beyond understanding or that feels overwhelming, ask God for a creation perspective. This may be through a picture in your mind, like the illustration of the grains of sand. It might be by reading the final chapters of Job and hearing them as God's words to you. Or it may be that you are able to go out and lean on a hundred-year-old gnarled tree and learn its lessons of survival, or stand on a cliff face and watch the never-failing constancy of the tide, or watch a storm where lightning illuminates the darkest sky.

Visual parables

Another way in which contemplating creation develops our relationship with the Creator is one which Jesus constantly modelled. Jesus often gave his most profound teaching in parables – parables about wheat and weeds, fish and nets, seeds and fruit, lilies and grass, sparrows and doves, fig trees and grapevines. As he was walking beside the lake or in the fields, Jesus noticed aspects of creation that were a wonderful starting point to reveal the truths of the kingdom.

When his disciples questioned him about why he spoke so often in parables, he gave this interesting answer: 'The reason I use parables in talking to them is that they look but do not see, and they listen, but do not hear or understand. So the prophecy of Isaiah applies to them: "This people will listen and listen, but not understand; they will look and look, but not see, because their minds are dull, and they have stopped up their ears and have closed their eyes. Otherwise their eyes would see, their ears would hear, their minds would understand, and they would turn to me, says God, and I would heal them."' (Matthew 13:13–15, GNB)

It seems that Jesus was suggesting that for most people the truths of the kingdom are not easily grasped because we resist seeing and hearing. Our hearts have become dull, our ears hard of hearing and our eyes are shut to what God wants us to see.

But Jesus had a way of creeping in under those defences with an illustration, a story or a parable – most often from the natural world visible to his hearers – and leaving the truth to dawn on them when they were ready. Sometimes he made the connections for them, sometimes he didn't.

If I say, 'Consider the lilies...', I'm sure most of you immediately call to mind Jesus reassuring his disciples that they have no need to worry (Matthew 6:25–34). If I mention 'the parable of the sower', even a person who is not a regular Bible reader is likely to recall that this is about different kinds of soil where seeds grow or fail to grow (Matthew 13:1–23). If I talk about 'faith like a mustard seed', at once a surge of encouragement is offered to faltering faith (Matthew 17:20). The truth of a visual parable seems to stick in the mind much longer and more effectively than a theological argument!

Ordinary things, things we can see, carry an enduring message for us once the connection has been made. Jesus used aspects of creation as illustrations of eternal truth so often that we are left in no doubt that we too are supposed to notice, and that we ourselves can learn to read the message the Creator has written for us. As we learn to walk meditatively and to look with a contemplative gaze, we will see our own illustrations, our own parables, personal messages from our creative God who longs to communicate with us at every turn.

A lovely example of a personal parable is expressed in the following poem by New Zealand writer Joy Cowley in her book *Aotearoa Psalms*. ('Aroha' is the Maori word for love.)

Shells

> *This morning we walked along a beach*
> *which seemed to be full of God's aroha.*
> *Sky, sea and sand, they were all alight,*
> *splash and dazzle, sparkle, shimmer,*
> *dancing in a celebration of love.*
>
> *Everything around us was praise.*
>
> *Then we came to a bed of shells.*
> *They were lying halfway between the tides,*
> *as neat as a parable.*
>
> *Some of the shells were turned up*
> *like cupped hands filled with gift.*
> *All that was beautiful in the day*
> *was contained in their openness.*
> *But others were turned face down*
> *with their backs to the celebration,*
> *enclosing nothing but their own darkness and emptiness.*
>
> *Light. Dark. Full. Empty.*
> *Open. Closed. Yes. No.*
> *It gave us something to think about*
> *as we continued along the beach.*

❊ Try it

I'm sure you can guess! Go out with eyes and heart open for God to show you parables in creation. When you see one, write it down. You don't have to be an accomplished poet! Treasure the parables God's Spirit helps you to notice because they will be of special significance for your personal journey.

Finally...

A beautiful Indian proverb says:

> *Love is revealed in words.*
> *When words are not enough,*
> *it is revealed in deeds.*
> *When deeds are not enough*
> *love resorts to music.*
> *Creation is the music of God.*

Listen to the music of God's love often!

CHAPTER 5
Pray without ceasing?

One of the most tantalising things the apostle Paul said was: 'Pray without ceasing' (1 Thessalonians 5:17). I wonder what your reaction is when you hear that? I can imagine a varied chorus of responses: 'Oh, I wish I could.' 'You've got to be joking!' 'What an awful standard to set – I'll always fail.' 'What on earth did you really mean, Paul?' 'Oh yeah... show me how!' 'It might be possible if you live in a monastery, but you obviously don't know my lifestyle!'

For many of us, life is busy. Days are filled with work, family responsibilities, church commitments, community events – it can seem like an endless cycle where we never quite catch up. Carving out quiet, uninterrupted time for meditative prayer is a big enough challenge, but praying all the time is surely asking a bit much!

I think interpreting Paul's words depends quite a lot on what we think prayer is. If prayer is about talking to God in a focused, concentrated way, then of course we can't do it unceasingly. We'd never get anything else done! If prayer always requires a quiet space in which to listen meditatively to God's Word, then we would need to live in seclusion to do that 'all the time'. Perhaps 'prayer' covers much more than we have ever thought.

Clement of Alexandria (c. 150 – c. 215) said: 'Prayer is keeping company with God.' I like that! Keeping company with God all the time would be a wonderful way to live. A contemporary writer, James Houston, speaking of his own experience, says: 'I began to see prayer more as a friendship than a rigorous discipline. It started to become more of a relationship and less of a performance.' What a difference to see prayer as a friendship, a growing relationship, rather than a performance. Perhaps now we can hear the intention of Paul's words: 'Be aware of God's constant friendship. Enter into relationship with God all the time, whatever you are doing.'

Seen this way, 'pray without ceasing' begins to sound like a wonderful invitation rather than an impossible task. Of course, there's still the question of how we develop the capacity to 'keep company with God' throughout all the other demands of our days.

If you have been trying out the ways of meditating on scripture and in creation that we have already talked about, you have laid a good foundation already. Like any human friendship, special intimate times together make it easier to stay in relationship when things get busy. Friends or partners who know each other well can communicate with a look across a crowded room or can sense what the other might need at a stressful time. Those who don't spend much time together to nurture their relationship won't be able to be 'in tune' with each other when the pressure is on.

It's the same in our relationship with God. Times set aside for deeper communication with God build an intimacy, a 'knowing of each other' that is the basis for relating prayerfully in the midst of many distracting demands. It works the other way, too! As we learn to be in touch with God throughout the day, we look forward to the pleasure of some time alone together. The two ways of relating encourage and stimulate each other.

Staying constantly tuned to the presence and friendship of God is something we can learn to do – but it does take practice!

Practising the presence of God

You may have heard the phrase 'practising the presence of God' before. It comes from the writings of a seventeenth-century French monk called Brother Lawrence. His conversations and letters were published in a little book called *The Practice of the Presence of God*.

Brother Lawrence did in fact live in a monastery. However, his was not a peaceful life with long hours of uninterrupted silence – he worked in the kitchen! Preparing meals for a large community and cleaning up afterwards is not naturally a contemplative lifestyle. Nevertheless, he learned how to do all his work with a deep inner awareness of God's presence so that eventually he could say: 'The time of business does not with me differ from the time of prayer; and in the noise and clutter of my kitchen, while several persons are at the same time calling for different things, I possess God in as great tranquillity as if I were upon my knees at the Blessed Sacrament.'

How did Brother Lawrence come to this place? And how can we learn to live like that? Brother Lawrence admits that at first it was hard. He says that it took ten years of practice before he could make the above statement. His aim was to carry out all his actions for the love of God, yet he found that frequently he would realise that he had forgotten God for long periods of time. Rather than get upset and frustrated when this happened, he would simply thank God that he was now reminded again of God's presence and go on in peace.

This quiet, persistent determination to practise being aware of the presence of God, without discouragement at his failures, brought Brother Lawrence to the point where he says: 'Thus, by rising after my falls, and by frequently renewed acts of faith and love, I am come to a state, wherein it would be as difficult for me not to think of God, as it was at first to accustom myself to it.'

What a wonderful place to arrive at! And it is just as possible for us as it was for Brother Lawrence. It is essentially a matter of training ourselves to be aware of the fact that God is present in every moment of our day. We do not make him any more present *than he already is*. But our *awareness* of God's presence enables us to enjoy him and all the fruits of the companionship he offers.

Pause for a minute and reflect on what practical difference it would make to your life if you were constantly aware of God's presence. If you have someone you can talk to about this, pose the question and discuss it. You might be surprised at how many areas of your life would be enriched, challenged or companioned!

The apostle Paul reminded his hearers at Athens that God is not far from each one of us. 'For "in him we live and move and have our being"' (Acts 17:28). Isn't that amazing? We don't have to go searching for God and wondering where to find him. He is right here, right now, in every moment of our life. God's presence is as available to us as the air we breathe! It is interesting that the Hebrew word *ruach* means both 'spirit' and 'breath'. Our physical life depends on the breath we breathe every moment of the day. We open our lungs to life-giving oxygen no matter what else we may be doing. Our spiritual life is 'oxygenated' by our openness to the presence of God, in whom we live and move and have our being.

Learning to be as open to the Spirit of God as we are to the air we breathe is a process. It is a process of becoming more and more aware of what actually is, rather than making something happen. It is waking up to what is already here.

Like Brother Lawrence and many other disciples of Jesus, we will each find our own ways of developing that awareness. There is no set formula, but below are some practical suggestions which you may find helpful.

Give your full attention to the present moment

This sounds deceptively simple, but how often do you find that your attention is distracted elsewhere, rather than focused on what's happening *now*? While listening to a sermon, you may be 'miles away', planning what to have for lunch or worrying about a financial problem. While bathing or playing with your children, you may *not* be focussing on them as much as on your frustration that you have so little time for yourself. While entertaining an unexpected guest, you may be present only in body while your mind races off, figuring out how to fit in the things you had planned to do at that time.

An alarming amount of our lives can pass by in this 'not present' way.

The problem with not being fully present to each moment is that we cannot enjoy God's presence in that moment because we are not really 'there' to enjoy it. The only moment we have to be aware of God's presence, and benefit from it, is the 'now' moment. This is such a profound truth that I wish I could emblazon it in sky-high letters!

Think about this for a minute from God's point of view. God is a loving, resourceful, caring friend who is present in every moment. He is not just 'up in heaven' or 'over there somewhere if I need him', but right within the depths of your being by his Spirit. 'The Spirit of God dwells in you' (Romans 8:9). All that God has to offer is available in every 'now' moment, but only in the now moment because that is the *only* moment we are experiencing. In my mind's eye I see God with countless gifts of encouragement, love, wisdom, courage, friendship, support, understanding, humour, comfort etc, offering just what is needed for each moment, but so often sadly putting the gift away again because we weren't 'there' to receive it.

✲ Try it

As often as you remember over the next few days, say to yourself, 'Right now I am (peeling potatoes, cleaning the bathroom, waiting at a red light) and this is a moment to enjoy God's company.'

Turn monologue into dialogue

Our minds are never completely void of thoughts. If you don't believe this, try to think of nothing at all right now. The constant 'mental chatter' that goes on in our heads can either help or hinder our awareness of God's presence.

Most of the time what we are saying to ourselves probably isn't very helpful. If you listen to your internal monologue, you may be surprised at how often it is negative. 'What did I say that for? Now everyone will think I'm stupid.' 'Oh I'm such an idiot! Why didn't I think of that?' 'Why didn't she smile at me? Have I upset her?' 'I feel so nervous about this interview I'll probably mess it up.'

Henri Nouwen (one of my favourite spiritual writers) calls this kind of thinking 'the graffiti of the mind'. One way of making our unceasing thoughts into unceasing prayers is to bring God into the conversation. 'Lord, I feel stupid after saying that. Help me.' 'Jesus, I'm upset that she didn't smile at me. What's going on?'

As you begin to do this, you will find that God has some replies to give. Remember, he is there in every situation. You may hear him say, 'I love you and I understand why it came out that way.' Or, 'Have you considered that she may be having a hard day and it's nothing to do with you?'

Turning monologue into dialogue not only makes us more aware of God's presence, it also safeguards us against unhelpful introspection and self-judgement.

As we make it more and more of a habit to include God in our internal conversations, we will discover that we are fulfilling two more of Paul's suggestions. We will 'take every thought captive to obey Christ' (2 Corinthians 10:5). I like the way *The Message* paraphrase expresses this: 'Fitting every loose thought and emotion and impulse into the structure of life shaped by Christ.' We are open to the perspective of Jesus on our thoughts and emotions. The result of this will be that we are being 'transformed by the renewing of [our] minds' (Romans 12:2).

✷ Try it

Over the next twenty-four hours, try to catch some of your internal monologue and deliberately turn it into dialogue with God. Be sure to listen for his side of the conversation!

Pray now, not later

During a busy day, how often do you think 'I must pray about that later'? And how often do you actually do it? For most of us, our intentions are better than our practice. But perhaps we overlook the fact that God doesn't need our carefully crafted words or long explanations in order to hear the prayers of our heart. A great deal of praying can be done the instant something comes to mind.

When you are interacting with someone, lift them up in your heart to God. When you are aware that you have sinned, confess it immediately rather than letting guilt mar the rest of your day. If something lovely happens, give thanks on the spot. If you need wisdom, ask for it as you are encountering the situation. In this way we can do a great deal of thanksgiving, adoration, confession and intercession in the course of a day.

Not only does this kind of praying take up no extra time, it also serves to keep us aware of God's immediate and intimate involvement in every aspect of the day.

Sometimes this kind of prayer can take a form similar to the nonverbal communication you have with friends. You can communicate volumes with a look across a room without using any words. Similarly, we can learn to offer to God many aspects of our day without the need for many words or even thoughts. God is well able to read the intention of our heart. Remember the encouragement of Romans 8:26,27 which assures us that even 'sighs too deep for words' are prayers that the Holy Spirit understands.

In time you will discover that the instinctive response to every situation is to turn towards God with your heart, your intention, your openness. With or without words, the whole of life becomes prayerful.

✷ Try it

As you read this section, you may have thought 'I already do this!'. Great! Maybe you 'pray without ceasing' more than you realised. Keep noticing how often during the day you simply lift your heart towards God in the midst of whatever is happening. Be grateful for such an ever-present friend!

Open yourself to God's resources for each task

If God is right there with us in every moment, with all the resources of the Spirit, it seems obvious that we should ask for them. But how often do we do it? Sometimes I find myself leaping in to a project or task, and only when I get stuck do I stop to ask God for advice. How much better it is when I take the time first to pause quietly and be open to the Spirit of God, breathing into my mind and heart the inspiration, the ideas, the wisdom that come from God. Often before I begin to write or prepare a sermon or seminar, I will go for a walk, opening myself to God's perspective on the topic in hand before I put my ideas on paper. Here is 'meditation on the move' again! I used to think going for a walk was a luxury and 'not really work', but I have discovered that it is one of my best ways to be open. After that kind of a walk, I sit down at my desk with the energy and flow of the Spirit to guide my work.

Brother Lawrence talks about how he would pray for God's grace and resources for each task and then, after completing it, evaluate how it went. If it had gone well, he thanked God. If not, he committed that to God too, if necessary asking pardon for his own mistakes and 'without being discouraged, he set his mind right again, and continued his exercise of the presence of God, as if he had never deviated from it.'

There is great wisdom here in leaving behind what is done and moving on without undue elation or recrimination. Of course, we will not always be so completely open to God that we float through each task with effortless success! We are in a lifelong process of staying in tune with the Spirit, and growth usually comes through both good times and bad. God is as compassionate with us when things go badly, as when they go well!

✽ Try it

Specifically commit some task you do today to God, asking for his resources and grace before you start. At the end of it evaluate how it went, commit the outcome to God and move on.

Celebrate the gift of monotony

Monotonous tasks that don't require much mental concentration can become gifts of space for enjoying God's presence, eg housework, doing the dishes, ironing, cleaning windows, driving, jogging, swimming, queuing at the supermarket or at traffic lights.

This is linked with giving your full attention to the present moment. Learn to say: 'Right now I am doing a pile of ironing and this is time I have to be aware of God's presence. I open myself to anything God may want to offer me.' The advantage of monotonous tasks is that there is usually quite a bit of time to stay open to what God offers.

When I lived in Nigeria, I remember one day facing the task of cleaning all the louvre windows in my house *yet again* as they became covered in dust in the dry season. Since my whole house had louvres, there were a lot of individual glass panes to be washed. I decided, pretty much on impulse, that on every pane I would chat to God about a different person I loved and cared about. That experience stands out in my memory as a time of wonderful friendship with God as we shared the joys and sorrows and needs of people we both loved.

A change of attitude makes a big difference to how we manage monotonous or repetitive tasks. The 'Oh no, not this again!' attitude is like breathing in stale air and sets us up for boredom and irritability. But it's quite possible (I've discovered!) to choose to breathe in the fresh air of the Spirit to transform your attitude. I might vacuum a floor covered with cat hair and be grateful to God for my furry companions and the joy they bring to my life. I'm even learning to sit in a traffic jam and simply accept that I can't change it, but that I'm here with God who is my friend and companion, so why not use the time to enjoy that!

* Try it

The next time you have a monotonous task to do, deliberately change your attitude by thanking God for the freedom it gives you to enjoy his company.

Choose a resting place for your mind

You may be thinking that putting into practice all these ideas could be quite exhausting. That is not the intention. You may find that one or other of the suggestions is enough to start with. Experiment with your own best ways of staying in touch with God's company and friendship. Remember that praying without ceasing is not a task to perform but an invitation to constant companionship.

One final suggestion is to get into the habit of having a 'home base' for your mind. This is a place you can return to often in the midst of a busy day. A good way to do this is to take a phrase of scripture, or a line of a song, or a word or image that you want to focus on. Let that be your anchor, keeping you steady and centred on Jesus. It may vary from day to day. It could be a key phrase from a recent meditation, or it may be a core truth that, once established, is a permanent resting place, eg 'The Lord is my shepherd' or 'Underneath are the everlasting arms'. It might be a prayer you can pray in one breath: 'I trust you'; 'Come Lord Jesus'. Or it might be a word you hear God saying to you: 'Peace, be still', 'I love you'.

It's helpful if your prayer phrase is short enough to flow naturally in rhythm with your breathing. Then, especially if you are feeling tense or rushed, you can breathe your prayer and feel its truth calming and relaxing you. This is a specially good way to combine breath for your body and breath for your spirit!

Once again words don't have to be the only way to do this. If you are a visual person, you may choose to ask the Spirit to give you a picture of a safe, peaceful place where God is always waiting to meet you. Then let your mind and heart go there often throughout the day and breathe in the peacefulness of the scene.

In time your resting place will become a deep undercurrent beneath all the busyness.

✶ Try it

Take a moment right now to choose a resting place for your mind. What would you most like to be the 'home base' you return to throughout the next day?

The fruit of it all

The amazing and wonderful fact is that there is no moment of our day or night when God is not present. The fruit of our growing awareness of this is a deepening intimacy with God in every aspect of life. We discover that 'keeping company with God' is not only possible, but is a coming home to how God always intended life to be.

The naked intimacy that Adam and Eve enjoyed with God reminds us of what God always wanted. Nothing hidden. Nothing separated from his presence. Jesus expresses that intimate presence again as he says: 'I am the vine; you are the branches. Those who abide in me and I in them bear much fruit, because apart from me you can do nothing' (John 15:5). The Jerusalem Bible translates 'abide in me' as 'make your home in me', so verse 4 reads: 'Make your home in me, as I make mine in you.' What a beautiful picture! What a wonderful reality! We are most at home in the presence of God in whom we live and move and have our being. And God has already made his home in the very heart of our being by his indwelling Spirit. Dwell on this profound truth. Relish it. Enter into it. Reverently and joyfully celebrate it. Home is right here, right now in God's company.

When we live from that centre the fruit will overflow beyond our own lives. Of Brother Lawrence it was said: 'His very countenance was edifying; such a sweet and calm devotion appearing in it, as could not but affect the beholders. And it was observed, that in the greatest hurry of business in the kitchen, he still preserved his recollection and heavenly-mindedness. He was never hasty nor loitering, but did each thing in its season, with an uninterrupted composure and tranquillity of spirit.'

However busy life is, when it is lived from our home in God, we can breathe in the life of God for every moment and breathe out God's grace and love to all we meet.

CHAPTER 6
When words won't do

We live in a very wordy world! Words spoken, words listened to; words read in books, papers, magazines; words written in assignments, letters, emails; words on billboards, TV screens, computer screens; words of instruction, words of persuasion; kind words, harsh words...

Words of course are a wonderful gift, enabling communication and learning. It is no accident that in speaking of the incarnation of Jesus, John wrote that 'the Word became flesh and lived among us' (John 1:14). God's communication, God's Word, was made tangible in the person of Jesus. Maybe right here we have the first clue that spoken words – or 'words on paper' – sometimes aren't enough for the deepest level of communication to take place.

God had spoken many words through the prophets and through his spokespeople in the Old Testament, but for many people the message didn't really get through until the word was made flesh, made real, made tangible in the person of Jesus. Words are an amazing tool which will take us just so far in understanding and communication. But sometimes words just aren't enough!

In human relationships we know how true this is. There are times when the depth of a feeling cannot be adequately verbalised. If no alternative channel is found, the feeling may be repressed or may leak out in ways that do not directly express its source. But, thankfully, words are not the only way to communicate. A lot can be said through eye contact, touch, actions or a symbolic gift. Messages of love, support, forgiveness, apology, surprise, delight can be 'given flesh' in ways that words alone could not convey. Of course it is also true that negative and hurtful messages can be given just as easily in non-verbal ways.

Communications experts tell us that we actually communicate seven times as much non-verbally as verbally. Think about that! What might you be 'saying' in all those non-verbal ways in an average day? Reflect on some recent incident to see this in reality. For example, a person can do the dishes angrily and grudgingly, conveying loud and clear (without words!) that it should be someone else's job. But the dishes can also be done peacefully and willingly, conveying pleasure in letting someone else have a rest from the task.

What is true in human relationships is also true in our relationship with God. Words are a wonderful communication tool, but there are times when words are not enough. And even when words are being used, there will be still more communication going on beneath the words. It is possible to read scripture hastily and grudgingly, conveying the message: 'I suppose I ought to do this, so let's get it done'. This is very different from reading with an eagerness and openness that communicates: 'I'm listening with anticipation, Lord'.

Reading the words of scripture will always be important. Verbalising our prayers to God out loud, in our mind or in written form in a journal will continue to be helpful and probably the main way we pray. But what do we do when somehow words fall short? Has prayer dried up? Has communication failed? Not necessarily! Maybe it is time to explore new channels; perhaps there are seven times as many ways to pray as well! In this chapter we will look at some of those non-verbal ways to pray.

Sighs too deep for words

> 'Likewise the Spirit helps us in our weakness; for we do not know how to pray as we ought, but that very Spirit intercedes with sighs too deep for words' (Romans 8:26).

One thing I love about the Bible is that it is so realistic. Here's a good example. Right in the middle of one of the most profoundly theological letters of the apostle Paul, he reassures us that sighs too deep for words are prayer too.

Eugene Peterson in *The Message* puts it this way: 'God's Spirit is right alongside helping us along. If we don't know how or what to pray, it doesn't matter. He does our praying in and for us, making prayer out of our wordless sighs, our aching groans.'

Isn't that amazing? A sigh, a groan, a heartfelt desire, is deeply understood by the Spirit of God and communicates far more than our faltering words could ever do. The scripture goes on to say: 'And

God, who searches the heart, knows what is the mind of the Spirit, because the Spirit intercedes for the saints according to the will of God' (Romans 8:27). Perhaps it's just as well we don't use words at times like this. Only the Spirit of God can read the deepest longing of our hearts and pray in us what truly matches the will of God.

In practice, what does this mean? How does this kind of prayer happen in ordinary life? I remember vividly an experience many years ago when a young member of my extended family was diagnosed with Hodgkins disease. A well-meaning and prayerful friend asked me what I was praying for the person concerned. I felt cornered and awkward because in a flash I realised that I wasn't actually praying anything in words or specific requests. It all seemed too big and overwhelming for that. I mumbled some kind of response, all the while feeling a very inadequate pray-er. I know now that what I was doing was groaning with sighs too deep for words and that God's Spirit understood the confusion, complexity and desire of my heart. What's more, that same Spirit turned all that into intercession on my behalf.

The prayer of 'sighs too deep for words' may also be part of much less dramatic and memorable occasions. A few days ago I was in the library and passed a mother with a six- or seven-year-old child. The child was desperately asking to be allowed to choose a book and the mother was angrily saying: 'I've come to get *my* books. We don't have time to go to the children's section.' My heart went out to that little girl, and I lifted her wordlessly to God. It was a fleeting moment in an ordinary day. I could not intervene but I could let my sigh become my prayer, and in doing so I believe my heart and God's heart connected.

This kind of wordless prayer is not confined to the sad and over-whelming situations of life. There can be sighs too deep for words that express wonder, awe and joy as well. I often begin the day with a walk along the beach near my home. Sometimes I 'chat to God' with specific thoughts, and there is a dialogue between us in my mind. But quite often I'm aware of a welling-up of delight and wor-ship which I cannot name. It's a relief to know that I don't have to spoil the moment by trying to put it into words. The Spirit reads my heart and wings my prayer to God.

I suppose one way to describe this kind of prayer is to say that it is simply a matter of learning to open your heart to God, of inviting the Spirit to be part of your feelings whatever they may be, even if you don't fully understand them yourself. That opening of the heart, that invitation to the Spirit, is what turns sighs into prayerful sighs. I could, of course, have witnessed the scene in the library and simply felt angry at the mother and worried about the child without opening myself to God at all. I'm sure God's heart would still have gone out to the child, but I would not have had a sense of connection with God or any constructive place to put my feelings. 'Lifting my heart to God' is the best way I know to express it briefly. A great deal of wordless prayer takes place as we grasp this wonderful opportunity to let the Spirit pray in us.

✶ Try it

As often as you can, notice your feelings and your sighs and simply lift them to God. Discover the freedom and relief of not having to put them into words. Be grateful that the Spirit prays on your behalf.

The prayer of the body

I'm sure you've heard people talk about 'body language'. It's an interesting phrase when you stop to think about it. In our everyday, colloquial speech, we are acknowledging the fact that bodies have a language of their own. This is another confirmation of the fact that we communicate more non-verbally than verbally.

In my work as a spiritual director, I often observe that a person's body is saying something quite different from their words. One person may smile brightly while telling of sad events. Another may stoically claim that everything is fine, while their brow is furrowed, their shoulders hunched and their hands tightly clenched. Sometimes a flush of colour indicates a depth of feeling which is not being spoken, and often tears will come unbidden to express a feeling as yet unnamed.

The body doesn't usually lie! Perhaps it is possible at times to put on a fake smile or try hard to look relaxed in the hope of convincing someone, but most of the time the body will speak its language much more loudly than we realise. Try watching a TV programme with the sound turned off. You will no doubt discover that you can tell a great deal about the mood, character and intentions of the cast by simply observing their body language.

I have a growing conviction that we don't use our bodies nearly enough in our prayer. Somehow, in our Western culture especially, we have relegated prayer to the mind and almost cut ourselves off at the neck when it comes to praying! We not only need to descend from the mind to the heart, but also to expand from the head to the rest of the body!

Once again, we are encouraged by many biblical examples.

- Miriam led the Israelites in a joyful dance after they had crossed the Red Sea (Exodus 15:20).

- Moses raised his hands in prayer as the Israelites fought (Exodus 17:8–16).

- Moses also lay prostrate before the Lord to plead for the forgiveness of the Israelites' sins (Deuteronomy 9:18).

- The Israelites marched a prayerful journey round the walls of Jericho for seven days (Joshua 6).

- David danced before the Lord with all his might (2 Samuel 6:14).

- The psalmists encourage us to bow down in worship (Psalm 5:7) and to lift up our hands in praise (Psalm 134:2).

- The humble body language of the tax collector spoke of his repentance (Luke 18:13).

- Jesus knelt in his agonising, sweating prayer in the garden of Gethsemane (Luke 22:41).

- The apostle John fell down in awe as God spoke to him (Revelation 1:17).

In some church cultures raising of hands, clapping or dancing is a recognised part of corporate worship. The freedom to use our bodies in this way is great, as long as it isn't imposed by worship leaders on those who prefer not to participate! In some churches we kneel to pray and stand to sing. Again, this is a good way of bringing our whole selves into the acts of worship. However, I suspect that often the physical postures are a routine that no longer hold a deep meaning for the participants. Perhaps a completely new physical action or posture might wake up a new level of meaning. For example, I wonder what would be stirred if we were invited to beat our breasts during the prayer of confession. Or how would it change our prayers of intercession if we lifted our hands as a sign of holding the people prayed for before God?

In the privacy of our personal prayer, it can be very freeing to let our bodies express our prayer. Simply thinking about what body posture would express how I am coming to God can be revealing.

- Am I coming tired and needing to curl up and be refreshed?
- Am I coming angry and needing to shake my fist at God as I express the truth of what is in me?
- Am I coming in awe and needing to lie prostrate before the Maker of the universe?
- Am I full of joy and wanting to put on some music and dance?
- Am I tense and stressed and needing to walk or jog my prayer with my whole body?

✷ Try it

You may be surprised at the depth to which your prayer will go if you let your body be an active participant. To lie curled up, as it were, in the arms of God as you express your tiredness can open new channels for God's refreshment. To put on a worship tape and dance your praise or your longing will take you far beyond what you could express in words. To pound out your anger or distress with your body will touch depths of emotion that need to be released and met with God's wise response. To lie prostrate as an indication of surrender and worship can become a deeply holy moment.

I encourage you to find your own rich ways of letting your body be a significant language of prayer.

A picture is worth a thousand words

We've all heard this saying, but I wonder if we've ever linked it to prayer. It seems that God does! Throughout the whole of scripture, God chooses again and again to communicate in pictures or visual symbols. They convey in tangible ways the profound reality that is often beyond mere words.

Imagine the impact of smearing blood on the doorposts of your house as a sign of God's protection (Exodus 12:13). Think of how you might respect the holiness of God if the most holy place was hidden by an ornately-worked curtain of 'blue, and purple, and crimson' (Exodus 26:31) and could only be entered by a priest at specific times. What might it be like to see a real goat led out into the desert after your sins had been named and symbolically placed upon it (Leviticus 16:20–22)?

God often spoke to the prophets in picture language. He asked: 'What do you see, Jeremiah?' and then gave him two symbolic pictures to explain the task before him (Jeremiah 1:11–15). Ezekiel's vision of the valley of dry bones coming to life communicated God's power and purpose graphically (Ezekiel 37). Amos was shown how far Israel had moved from God in a picture of God's plumb line (Amos 7:7–9).

The psalms are full of picture images to help us grasp the nature of God and our relationship to him. We are invited to be 'like a tree planted by the water' (Psalm 1:3). God is described as a shepherd (Psalm 23), as having sheltering wings (Psalm 61:4), as a rock of refuge (Psalm 62:7), as our sun and shield (Psalm 84:11) and so on.

Even though the biblical writers are using words to tell us of their pictures or symbols, in the first instance the pictures spoke their own message to the prophet or psalmist. Jesus encouraged his followers to 'see' God in this way too. He pointed out fields of wheat and weeds, or a wounded sparrow, or lilies in a field, or fish in a net and asked the 'What do you see?' question. Jesus described himself in symbolic terms as a door, a vine, a light, a way. Each picture conjures up associations that lead us to a fuller knowledge of who Jesus is. Perhaps the ultimate symbolic picture Jesus wanted us to remember is the meaning of bread broken and wine poured out. Although words were intertwined with the visual images, even without them the visual stimuli convey the message powerfully.

I'm sure you are getting the idea that visual and symbolic communication is a big part of God's repertoire. I've only picked out a few examples. There are many more!

Once again, it's worth asking: how does this expand the ways I can pray? Let me suggest some I have found useful. We've touched on one of them already in chapter 4. Learn to let God's whole creation be part of his non-verbal communication. Get in the habit of hearing the 'What do you see?' question and allowing the visual parables all around you to be received.

Another way of using visual images as a way of prayer is to use colour and drawing or painting to express your heart to God. This is not about being an artist (although that would be a bonus!), it is simply a different channel through which to communicate. I know some people whose journals are full of sketches, diagrams, colour and collage. These express what is in the depth of their being more fully than words. I'm sure God loves to receive such creative, colourful communication.

When I'm accompanying someone on their spiritual journey and they are finding it hard to put into words what's happening, I will often say: 'Choose a colour that seems to match what you're feeling and put a shape or a symbol on the page.' (I always have paper and pastels close by!) Even when the idea seems strange and the person may protest 'I don't know how to do this', it's amazing what emerges as they simply let the colour and shape express what they cannot name. Sometimes words and emotions are released by the act of drawing. Sometimes the drawing grows to express far more than they knew was there, and may or may not need to be explained in words.

✳ **Try it**

You can use loose paper and pastels or crayons, or get a blank page scrapbook to use as your visual prayer journal. Here are some ideas to get you started.

- As you come to a time of prayer, choose one or more colours that match how you are feeling today. Put the colours on the page with shapes or symbols that seem to express your feelings, eg joyful swirls, angry scribbles, peaceful, flowing lines. Now choose a God colour and ask God to show you where and how he is in the picture. Let God's presence be expressed on the page too.

- Doodle or diagram your prayer. Let the things you are trying to sort out with God be expressed on paper. Perhaps you feel trapped by some situation. Draw yourself in the trap. Ask God for his ideas about how to be free. Draw the possibilities.

- Sketch a picture of where you and God are in relation to each other. Are you close together or far away? Is God facing you with open arms or is he way out ahead calling you to follow? Are you resting in God's embrace or hiding your face in your hands, afraid to look? Now ask God to show you the picture he sees. Draw the way God wants to relate to you in love. Pray for the grace to let him meet you that way.

Drawing is not the only way to have a 'picture worth a thousand words'. Noticing and choosing symbols to put in your place of prayer is another way to keep you close to God, using a visual channel. I recently went to a toy shop and bought one of those little round toys that has a weight in the centre so when you push it over it always pops back up. It was my symbol of wanting to stay so centred in God that even the knocks and bumps of life would not push me off balance. As I walk past the toy I give it a playful push and smile as it bounces back. No one who happened to see me would guess I was praying!

✷ **Try it**

Ask yourself right now: 'What symbol would sum up what I want to keep in touch with at the moment?' Then see if you can find or create that symbol and put it somewhere you will see it often.

Tangible, symbolic actions can bring what was once theory into an experienced reality. I remember once agonising with a friend who knew she was forgiven for past events but somehow couldn't feel the freedom of forgiveness. After many long, tearful discussions we hit on the idea of a tangible expression of her willingness to believe she was forgiven and to let go of the cloud of guilt that held her back. She wrote what she wanted to let go of on a piece of paper and we burnt it in the roasting pan out of the oven, safely placed on the breadboard to avoid scorching the carpet. That symbolic action brought a peace no theological discussion had achieved. A roasting pan and a breadboard were our prayerful altar that night.

✷ **Try it**

Experiment with your own ways of letting visual and symbolic images link you with God. The possibilities are endless. Words may or may not flow in and out of the visual symbols, but remember more is communicated non-verbally than verbally – and that's true of our prayer too.

✷

I expect it is abundantly clear by now that non-verbal prayer can be rich and full. It can supplement words or replace them altogether. It can open up channels of communication that take us to new places with God and it reassures us that God hears our sighs, reads our body language and delights to give and receive creative visual and symbolic messages. I hope you will enjoy the possibilities of these ways of 'deepening the roots of prayer'.

CHAPTER 7

The sound of sheer silence

There's one more aspect of non-verbal prayer to visit, and it deserves a chapter of its own! It is the place of 'sheer silence'. You will remember the story of Elijah fleeing to Mount Horeb in his exhaustion and discouragement, and sheltering in a cave while wind, earthquake and fire raged outside. As scripture puts it: 'the Lord was not in the wind; and after the wind an earthquake, but the Lord was not in the earthquake; and after the earthquake a fire, but the Lord was not in the fire; and after the fire a sound of sheer silence' (1 Kings 19:11,12). Various translators of scripture tried different ways of expressing how God met Elijah that day. The Jerusalem Bible says God came 'in the sound of a gentle breeze'. The NIV calls it a 'gentle whisper' and the well known King James translation says there was 'a still small voice'. They all give a feel for something very special happening after all the noise died down.

It seems paradoxical to speak of the *sound* of sheer *silence*. Yet I imagine you know something of what Elijah experienced. If you have been subjected to loud and continuous noise for a period of time and it suddenly stops, you really can 'hear' the silence. Silence is something you only notice when the noise stops, and when it does the silence speaks volumes.

Entering the place of prayerful silence is an important part of our spiritual journey. There are times when even the otherwise helpful 'techniques' of verbal and non-verbal prayer are an intrusion. What is most necessary then, is to let everything else fall away and be embraced by the sheer silence of God's love. However wonderful that sounds, it is often not easy to do. Let's take a look at why that might be.

I think there are two main reasons why silence is difficult for many people. The first is that when the noise and distraction of external events is removed, we discover there is a great deal of noise on the inside! It can be disconcerting to find thoughts and emotions welling up which we thought we had kept at bay. Sometimes they are merely annoying, repetitive distractions. Sometimes what emerges into the silence are things we would much prefer not to pay attention to. Deep down we are often afraid of what might be revealed in our own depths if we really entered the silence.

While such fears need to be met with understanding and compassion, it would be a great pity if we let them keep us from meeting God in the deep, silent places. As Elijah discovered, God was there at his most discouraged, fearful place, to meet him with new perspectives and encouragement.

So it can be that a prayerfully silent space becomes an entry point into a different kind of encounter with God than we expected. But what rich healing and wisdom is at hand when we let the deepest parts of ourselves listen to the 'still small voice' of God.

The second reason many of us find prayerful silence difficult is quite different. It is not about wanting to avoid what might be there. It is the uncomfortable suspicion that there's nothing there! The feeling is that it's pointless, a waste of time, because 'nothing happens'. In the past week I have listened to two people who, unknown to each other, both said that at the moment their best 'God space' was sitting in the sun by a window just 'soaking in God's love'. Both of these people were hesitant about whether this could really be prayer because, as one said, 'I'm not doing anything. I'm just being there.' The other person's main concern was, 'I'm not even using words any more.'

Most of us are immersed in a culture that emphasises productivity, being useful, getting things done, having something to show for it, not wasting time. This unconsciously carries over even into our prayer. It is easy to think that prayer should be productive. I should be able to tick off on a list what I've done in my prayer today. If I've spent time with God, I should have something to show for it. If asked, I should be able to say 'what happened'.

When this is how we (perhaps unconsciously) operate, the thought of just being quietly in the presence of God without any preconceived agenda seems like a waste of time. But think again. Can being in the presence of God ever be a waste of time? There is mystery here, for it is true that it may indeed seem as if 'nothing happens'. Yet on the level of God's Spirit meeting our spirit, we can trust that far more is 'happening' than we will ever know.

Throughout the centuries men and women of prayer have encouraged those seeking deeper connection with God to practise the simplest, yet hardest, discipline of all: sit in your cell (or your room) and be silent. Prayerful silence is a strand woven into every era of spirituality. We should not be surprised. After all, it was God's idea in the first place! Through the psalmist God reminded his people that they needed to 'be still and know that I am God' (Psalm 46:10). If you read the whole psalm, you will see that it is a psalm about uproar and tumult in the nations and in the world. That is the very point at which it is so important to be still, be quiet and let a different kind of 'knowing' take hold.

Here are some of the ways we may begin to do this.

Finding the still centre

Without some measure of solitude and silence it is impossible to find, beneath all the fragmented parts of our lives, the still centre where God dwells. It is as if we live on the windswept turbulent surface of life and never dive into the deep stillness of God. We sometimes speak of needing to 'get myself together'. A very telling phrase! So much of the time we are fragmented, not really 'all here'. Silence and solitude provide the opportunity to be still and let all the turbulence subside, and to begin to sense a coming home to ourselves and to God.

An old proverb says: 'Muddy water, let stand, becomes clear'. Sometimes the very best use of silence is simply to let ourselves be, until the whirling thoughts, pressures and anxieties have a chance to settle. Then perhaps there will be a clear enough space to be aware of God and his gentle understanding and love.

The fruit of this kind of silence will be a greater calmness and focus as we go about the rest of our day.

* Try it

Some time in the next day or two, when you feel frazzled, fragmented and in need of 'getting yourself together', find a place where you can be alone and quiet. Then just sit there and imagine yourself as a jar of stirred-up, muddy water. Stay still and quiet until you sense the whirling debris sinking to the bottom and a clear space forming. You don't have to do anything or work anything out. Just be still and remember that God is God!

Planned availability

When we are busy with specific tasks or even specific prayer agendas, we are not fully available to listen to God. To be available in this way means handing over our control of the time and waiting with a heart attuned and eager to hear the voice of God – or the silence of God.

In silence we begin to realise how much we like to be in control. We may discover that we are willing to spend time in silence if God 'says something', but quickly become restless and impatient if nothing seems to be happening. But perhaps God simply wants our company and love. Are we willing to be available for that too? What is it like for you to think that God might just want your company with no particular agenda other than lovingly being there?

Often, however, times of silence and solitude are times when God is able to bring to our minds issues or ideas he wants to communicate. Many people today are asking, 'How do I hear the voice of God?' The first and most basic answer is: stop talking, be quiet and listen!

Times of planned availability to listen, or to love and be loved by God, are often best placed after a time of biblical meditation. In fact, if you recall, the final step of *Lectio Divina* is contemplation – a silent resting in God's love. But as with any people who love each other, there is no limit to the times and places when such loving listening can take place!

✷ Try it

Plan a time when you can be available to God in this way. Maybe this will be by extending the time of silence after a biblical meditation, or maybe it will be a special time to simply be open to receiving God's love. Let God know that if he wishes to speak to you in this time you are listening. But if not, you are available to be with him anyway.

Humility

If you have tried out the suggestions so far, you will probably have discovered that to relinquish control, even in our prayer, does not come naturally. Our desires to 'do something', 'say something', 'have something to show for it', are all reflections of our strong need to control, to perform, to be in charge.

Silence and solitude reveal our pride very quickly. We need to learn the reality that it is only as we let go of our pride and our control that God can work in us. Perhaps this is at least one meaning of the first beatitude: 'Blessed are the poor in spirit, for theirs is the kingdom of heaven' (Matthew 5:3).

Spending time with God in silence is probably one of the best ways to 'deny ourselves', something Jesus repeatedly tells his disciples to do. In silent prayer we deny (set aside) our own cleverness, our own ideas, our own agendas, our own pet projects or pet gripes. In effect we say: 'Lord, I know that my perspectives are, at best, limited, and probably distorted as well. I let them all go now for this time of silence. I acknowledge that you are in control.'

Self-discovery

As we said earlier, one of the reasons some people avoid silence and solitude is that intuitively we know that to cut out all distractions means that we will be left facing ourselves.

It is true that in silence and solitude the surface layers of ourselves drop away and we confront deeper, more hidden realities. This need not be fearful or unpleasant of course, but sometimes it does take courage to discover at a deeper level what is going on inside us.

All the great writers on prayer insist, however, that without self-knowledge we cannot progress very far in knowing God. The basic reason is that if I am afraid to know myself, then I won't want to get too close to God because he might show me something I don't want to know. And if I keep my distance from God, then of course I can't get to know him very well either!

A most important thing to remember is that in prayerful silence, whatever surfaces, does so in the context of God's companionship and love. The more we are willing to let God show us who we are, the more we can allow him to love those aspects of ourselves. This, in turn, means that we become more whole, more integrated and more available to God and to others.

*⃰ Try it

Is your heart's desire to know God more deeply? If so, are you willing to know yourself more deeply in the light of his love? If your answer is yes, let silence be one of the ways you humbly allow this to happen.

The prayer of the heart

Through the centuries of Christian history, finding ways to enter prayerful silence has been a continuing theme. One of the most well-practised ways of doing so has been sometimes called 'the prayer of the heart' and sometimes 'centring prayer'. These are good descriptions because entering deeply into silence is like descending from the busy wordiness of our mind into the heart of our being. When we learn to do this, we find we can become centred and still.

We'll conclude this chapter by revisiting this well-tried route into prayerful silence. There are some simple steps outlined below, but first a contemporary image may help. Imagine getting into a lift on the top floor of a building and gliding down to the floor below. The top floor is a busy place with much activity. It is productive, organised and humming along with many projects on the go. There are offices with secretaries, filing cabinets, computers and photo-copiers. At its best this floor, the 'mind floor', is smooth-running, efficient and streamlined. Sometimes, though, when the pressure is really on, it becomes a frantic, disorganised and stressful place to be.

The contrast between the top floor and the one below is marked. When you emerge at the 'heart floor', the first thing that strikes you is the quietness. It takes a few minutes to adjust to the transition. There's a strange tranquility here. No rushing footsteps, no buzzing machines, nobody tapping at a computer keyboard. The foyer you step into from the lift is carpeted and has some easy chairs. It seems the invitation is to sit for a while and let yourself settle in this new atmosphere. As you relax and look around, you notice that this floor is open-plan. Beyond the foyer is a central area with two chairs facing each other. That's all there is. Somehow you know that if you cross the threshold and sit in one of the chairs, you will be joined by One who knows you through and through without you having to explain anything.

It is both inviting and frightening to descend from the mind into the heart. Tranquillity, silence and having 'nothing to do' but just be there is a strange new experience. Leaving behind the control we felt we had with many words and much activity can feel vulnerable. Being joined in the silence by the One who knows us through and through brings both relief and dismay. But if we have the courage to sit quietly with the ever-present, all-seeing God, we will discover more and more clearly that his name is Love.

Of course we don't really leave our mind behind when we enter the silence and create some centred heart space, but we do learn not to be caught up in its ceaseless busyness. One very helpful way to do this is to choose a simple, short prayer phrase for our mind to focus on. This centres our attention and leaves room for the spacious silence to expand our heart and spirit. A phrase like 'Come, Lord Jesus' or 'Peace, be still' can allow our mind to cooperate with our heart's desire for that silent communion with God beyond the words.

✷ Try it

1   Make sure you won't be interrupted and can sit or kneel in a comfortable, relaxed but alert posture.

2 Take some time to make the descent from the busyness of 'the top floor' of your mind. This may simply be by letting your body come to real stillness and by letting your breathing slow down. It may be helpful to visualise the journey down in the lift and see yourself sitting quietly in the carpeted foyer.

3 Choose a word or phrase that sums up your desire at the present time, eg 'Peace, be still', 'Come, Lord Jesus', 'Lord, have mercy', 'God, my all', 'Love', 'Peace', 'Jesus' etc.

4 Let your mind gently repeat that phrase while your whole being is simply 'being there' in the presence of the God who knows and loves you through and through. If you find your mind wanders (and it probably will!), simply return to the prayer phrase without anxiety.

5 Stay in this rhythm as long as you are able and willing – from ten to twenty minutes is a good amount of time.

6 When it is time to move on, do so with gratitude for this oasis of heart space, knowing you can return here again.

The last word

I've used quite a few words to talk about silence! In the end, the words and ideas are only signposts inviting you to discover for yourself the riches of God's love in the place beyond words. Let the last word be God's own invitation to 'be still and know that I am God'. Let him meet you in the stillness with 'the sound of sheer silence'.

CHAPTER 8
A rainbow-coloured relationship

There are so many ways to pray! Our relationship with God can be expressed, deepened and enjoyed through a rich variety of channels. In this book we've covered some of them. Many factors affect the way we choose to pray. Some of these might be: our life situation – busy or relaxed; our particular needs at a given time; how long we have been on the Christian journey; what we have been taught about how to pray, and so on.

One of the factors that may affect the way we pray more than we realise, is our personality. I vividly remember a student I had in my spiritual formation class at Bible college, who was secretly feeling a failure at prayer, because in her mind 'real prayer' meant having deep internal communication with God when alone and silent with eyes closed. When we talked about meditation on the move and ways of praying in the midst of daily activities, a light went on! A few weeks later, with eyes shining, she told me she now had wonderful prayer walks down in the orchard where she could talk out loud to God, keeping her eyes open to see all the beauty around her, and come back with her body, mind and spirit all in touch with God. She had discovered ways of praying that matched her personality. Even now, many years later, if I meet her, she will remind me of how life-changing that discovery was.

Personality and prayer is a tricky topic! It is all too easy to create categories which imply that if this is your personality, then this is how you will pray. That's far too limiting. It is also unfair to the breadth of personality and the mystery of prayer. However, our personality *does* influence the ways we most readily relate to God. So to be aware of that can be freeing and helpful.

There are two principles to keep in mind as we think of how our personality affects our prayer and spiritual life. One is the freedom to find and enjoy the ways of relating to God that are consistent with our personality. The other is to realise that as we get to know God better, there are treasures to be found beyond our 'comfortable' way of praying.

Think of it this way: when light shines through a prism, a rainbow of colours is revealed. There is a rainbow of ways in which God longs to communicate with us. Each of us will respond more readily to some colours of the rainbow because that is where our personality draws us. And that's where we can begin, enjoying fully God's light in the colours of our personality. But how exciting to realise that we are not limited to those colours only. We can open ourselves to new ways of praying, dust off little-used facets of the prism until the full rainbow of God's light is shining.

To explore this more fully, I'm going to use the four areas of personality preference that have long been observed as common to people regardless of culture, gender or way of life. Carl Jung wrote about them, and so did the mother-and-daughter team Katharine Briggs and Isabel Briggs Myers. Many of you will have heard of the Myers Briggs Type Indicator (MBTI®) developed by Katharine and Isabel and later validated by educational researchers in the USA. It is now a widely used tool to help people understand themselves and others and to enhance relationships. Isabel Briggs Myers called the book she wrote about it *Gifts Differing* (I B Myers Consulting Psychologists Press, 1980), to express the conviction that personality differences are gifts to be appreciated.

As we apply these areas of preference to the ways we pray and relate to God, it is not necessary to have completed an MBTI® programme (though if you have, so much the better). We will simply use this framework as a way to explore the many facets of what is possible as our relationship with God matures and grows.

The four areas where people instinctively have different preferences are:

- **Extraversion (E) and Introversion (I).** This is about where we get our energy. Extraverts are energised by the world around them. They are stimulated and inspired by the people and events they are involved with. Introverts find their energy is recharged when they have time to be quiet and away from the rush and bustle. Their energy comes from within and will surface best when they are alone with few distractions.

- **Sensing (S) and Intuition (N).** This is about how we take in information. Those with a sensing preference are tuned in to the specific information gained by their five senses. They notice details and are aware of the concrete steps in a process. Intuitives by contrast take in the big overall picture before they notice details. They will get a global view and make many connections without worrying too much about a step-by-step approach. Sensing people are good at living in the present and enjoying what is here and now. Intuitives are usually imagining future possibilities and reaching out for what could be better.

- Thinking (T) and Feeling (F). This is about how we prefer to process the information we have taken in and thus make decisions. Thinkers like to take a logical approach, work out the just way to make a decision and act on it with objectivity, however they may personally feel. People with a feeling preference start from a 'personally involved' position and make decisions based on the values they hold to be important. They want a decision to be fair to everyone and will consider the impact on each person to be an important factor in the best choice to make.

- Judging (J) and Perceiving (P). This is about the kind of lifestyle we prefer. People with a judging preference like things to be well organised and to know in advance what is expected. They will probably be disciplined in their own schedules and enjoy completing what they set out to do. People with a perceiving preference like to be spontaneous and let things develop without tying them down too tightly. They like to leave space for the unexpected and are often good at adapting to last-minute changes of plan.

We will each prefer to operate from one side of each pair. Of course we can, if necessary, use the other way of being and, when situations demand it, we may have learned to do so quite well. But it will feel more stressful than doing what comes naturally. Putting together the four preferences will give you a four-letter shorthand for your natural way of living out your personality. I prefer INFJ ways of being! I've learned to cope pretty well with the opposites – one at a time, anyway! But if I'm asked to do something which requires using all my non-preferences at once, I'm likely not to do too well and certainly will be exhausted at the end.

When it comes to our spiritual life, it's much the same. If we are trying to live a spiritual life based on preferences quite different from our own, it probably feels like an uphill journey, exhausting and not very joyful. What a relief to realise that the personality God has given you is the way he loves to relate to you. When you've really grasped that and your relationship with God is secure and growing, there will be energy and curiosity to motivate exploring some other colours of the rainbow!

Jesus is a wonderful role model. I'm sure he had preferences like every other person. Yet, as a perfectly developed human being, he was able to use all eight of the preferences appropriately as each situation demanded. Jesus' life was one in which God's light shone fully with all the colours of the rainbow!

Exploring the rainbow

An active relationship (E)

'Let your light shine' (Matthew 5:16).

Remember that extraverted people find their energy and inspiration primarily from interaction in the world of people and events. Active involvement in Christian service makes their spirituality come alive. Extraverts' spiritual growth and prayer are enhanced by the stimulus of external challenges and people to share with. They will naturally incorporate prayer in the activities of daily life, but may have a harder time settling down alone to quiet times of meditation.

Extraverts like to talk about what they are thinking and learning, clarifying new discoveries as they do so. Many extraverts say they don't really know what they think until they have a chance to verbalise it in discussion.

Corporate worship and praying with others are usually welcomed by extraverts (though it's quite possible to have a shy extravert, so don't put people in a box here). However, times of silent reflection in a church service or home group may feel uncomfortable, boring and far too long! As for going on a silent retreat or quiet day of prayer... for most extraverts this is likely to be quite daunting or even terrifying at first thought.

The gift of extraversion is a capacity to love God actively in the midst of life and among people. Extraverts meet God as they live life to the full and are happy to talk about the discoveries and challenges of the spiritual journey as they go along.

Much of Jesus' life was very extraverted. He was constantly interacting with people and responding physically and spiritually to their needs. We hear him calling on God in the midst of his public tasks: calming the sea; praying as Lazarus was raised; giving thanks for loaves and fishes. Much of the time I don't think Jesus delivered carefully prepared sermons from written notes! He spoke out the truth of God as he walked around and met people in new situations.

The pitfall extraverts have to watch out for is that they may find it hard to settle into quiet listening to God. There are always so many interesting things to get involved with that disciplined time to stop, be still and listen may get short changed.

If you recognise that you have an extraverted preference, delight in that! Use your active ways of loving God to the full. Pray out loud even when you're on your own if you want to. Link up with a good home group or discussion group where you can stretch your faith as you grapple with new ideas or the challenges you face on your journey. Find a specific sphere of service that will both challenge and energise you as you offer your personality to God. And be aware that there are rich gifts to be discovered in choosing to be a bit more introverted sometimes!

A reflective relationship (I)

'Be still and know that I am God' (Psalm 46:10).

Many books on prayer sound as though they were written by introverts, for introverts! Titles like *The Inner Journey, Deeper into God, The River Within* and *Thoughts in Solitude* sound inviting to introverts, but daunting to extraverts! Introverts find the invitation to 'be still and know that I am God' something they respond to eagerly. For them silence, stillness, space and solitude are the conditions that make it easiest to be receptive to God.

An introvert needs time to mull over new thoughts and spiritual discoveries on their own before being asked to share in a group, and if no one does ask them, they may not share at all. The spiritual life of an introvert is quite private. Their inner sanctuary is a holy place not open to everyone. However, an introverted person will value some close friends or a mentor with whom to share at depth what is most important.

In public worship an introvert will value times of quiet reflection (though they probably never feel long enough). A church service that is filled with words, high energy music and lots of active participation can feel draining and may even seem to make it harder to meet God deeply.

The gift of introversion is a capacity to find God within. Whether or not there is external stimulus, the introverted person can find ways to connect with the energising Spirit of God in their innermost being. From that place a deep, quiet wisdom is a gift they can share.

As Christians we know that the Spirit of God dwells within. In order to listen to the promptings of the Spirit, we need to withdraw from the noise and distraction of the world and make space for the voice of God to be heard. Jesus repeatedly withdrew to a quiet place to pray alone. He also instructed his disciples to go into their room and close the door to pray. *The Message* paraphrase expresses it: 'Find a quiet secluded place so you won't be tempted to role-play before God. Just be there as simply and honestly as you can manage. The focus will shift from you to God, and you will begin to sense his grace' (Matthew 6:6).

The pitfalls an introverted person needs to watch out for are that they may miss out on the challenge, fellowship and combined wisdom of others because they prefer to withdraw to their private place. They may also forget to let the rich fruit of their inner sanctuary be expressed in the outer world to nourish and serve others.

If you recognise that you have an introverted preference, be at peace! God welcomes you in the quiet, inner place. Go there often and take the time you need to allow the silence to deepen and the Spirit's insights to be given. Trust God to show you ways that the fruit of those times can be shared. Remember too that God may meet you richly as you stretch beyond your comfort zone and get involved in more extraverted ways!

A down-to-earth relationship (S)

'Taste and see that the Lord is good' (Psalm 34:8).

People with a sensing preference are straightforward, in touch with reality, living in the present moment and aware of all that there is to see, hear and take in with their five senses. A practical spirituality is important for them. Too many abstractions and theories take them away from simple attentiveness to God in the here and now. The phrase 'the sacrament of the present moment' applies well to sensing people.

In prayer they will find it helpful to pray simply and directly with specific requests for themselves and others. Music, a candle, a cross or some other sensory focus may be important to a sensing person in their prayer place. Praying in creation with all senses alert to God's world will be natural and enjoyable. Sensing people are good at 'seeing God in all things'. Listening to God and obeying in practical ways is a part of their discipleship.

The gift of a sensing person is their down-to-earth, practical approach to serving and getting things done. They model for others how to be content in the here and now, and how to find God in all things.

All of the qualities we have just described are true of Jesus too.

- He was very present to each moment and to the presence of God in that moment. He encouraged people to recognise God in the things that they could see and hear, touch and taste: 'Consider the lilies'; 'A sower went out to sow...'; 'Don't put a light under a barrel'; 'You are the salt of the earth'.

- Jesus was also a humble servant. Washing the disciples' feet and cooking breakfast for them on the beach were acts of his loving service in practical ways.

- In his own prayer he listened attentively to God and obeyed. He says that he did nothing by himself but only what the Father showed him (John 5:19).
- He gave very specific practical instructions to his followers: 'Turn the other cheek'; 'Take up your bed and walk'; 'Go and show yourself to the priest'; 'Go home and tell your family'.

The pitfalls a sensing person needs to watch out for are that they may limit their awareness of God to what is tangible, practical and obvious. Paradoxes and mysteries may be dismissed as distractions.

If you recognise that you have a sensing preference, be glad! Enjoy your ability to see God in all things. Simple, straightforward honesty and obedience will keep you close to God. The world needs a down-to-earth gospel. You bring the love of Jesus to people where they are through your active, practical service. Don't forget, though, that the colours of mystery and paradox are God's colours too!

A mysterious relationship (N)

'Faith is ... the conviction of things not seen' (Hebrews 11:1).

People with an intuitive preference are always looking for the big picture. They are tuned in to possibilities, to change, to visions of the future. They have a great capacity to imagine and to dream. For them, relationship with God offers hope for change and newness of life. There is often a great desire to grow beyond the now and to experience more than they have so far discovered.

Mystery and questions are familiar territory for an intuitive person. In fact, if there is nothing to question, an intuitive will probably create some new ones! Intuitive people are often creative and like to explore their spirituality through music, art, dance, drama, story or symbol. They will long for corporate worship to reflect this variety and creativity.

In private prayer they may get bored quite quickly with one way of spending time with God and need the freedom to try new things. Intuitives also need plenty of time to be quietly with God without a fixed agenda. Their musing with God may flit from one thing to the next as connections are made and significant insights emerge.

The gift of the intuitive person is their confidence in what is possible and their creative ways of reaching out for more.

God is a God of vision, possibility and change. His creativity is obvious in every aspect of our universe. Prophetic future thinkers are key people throughout the scriptures. Jesus was sometimes seen as an unrealistic dreamer. His way of looking at life was often scorned or misunderstood by the law-abiding Jew. He saw beyond what was obvious and what was fixed in people's minds as 'the way things are'. Jesus used symbol and story to encourage others to see a bigger picture. The parables are a good example. His use of the bread and wine to symbolise his death and resurrection keeps a central mystery of the gospel before our eyes. Paradox and mystery are woven throughout Christianity. We are relating to a holy and majestic God, and that means accepting that there is always a reality bigger than what we can see right here.

The pitfall intuitive people need to watch out for is the tendency to overlook or ignore practical, present realities! They may also leave others a bit confused by their constant desire for change and innovation.

If you have an intuitive preference, relish it! Be thankful for your capacity to dream and to imagine what could be. We need a prophetic, dreaming church. We need people with a vision of the kingdom of God that encourages us to trust 'what we do not see'. We need those who can live with paradox and mystery. But keep your feet on the ground as well. Learn to let the practical, sensing realities inform and anchor your dreams.

A thoughtful relationship (T)

'The truth will make you free' (John 8:32).

People with a thinking preference want to be assured of a God who is transcendent, just and reliable. Issues of truth and justice are very important to them. Their faith needs a firm foundation of reasoned thought and a coherent theology.

In their personal times of prayer and devotion, a systematic approach to Bible study is likely to be important and fruitful. Thinkers are able to grapple with the tough issues and, if necessary, argue with God about them. One thinker says, 'I am a natural sceptic. I came to faith by arguing with God and losing, just as Paul did.' (B Duncan, *Pray your way: your personality and God*, DLT, 1993.)

In public settings intelligent, well thought-out preaching or discussion is important to a thinker. They will ask lots of questions and want to understand thoroughly the underlying principles of Christian belief. Vague generalisations will not do. People with a thinking preference will generally feel that public settings are not the place for personal and emotional issues to be on display.

Thinkers bring the gift of thoughtful depth to a Christian community. They will challenge fluffy thinking and ask the hard questions that bring muscle to our discipleship.

It is easy to see how thinkers represent some very important aspects of the image of God. God is a God of truth. The truth about life and about God is anchored and demonstrated in the scriptures. These can be studied with all the rigour of top academic scholarship. We do not need to be afraid that God will not stand up to questions! One of the things we see clearly throughout scripture is that justice is a primary passion for God. This is an aspect of God's character that thinkers share.

Deeply understood principles for life and faith are demonstrated well in the life of Jesus. Consider how cleverly he challenged the legalistic thinking of the Pharisees and taught God's ways at a much deeper level, for example in the Sermon on the Mount. There was an assertive strength in Jesus that met challenge with clarity and confidence. For example, he did this in his response to the temptations, the question about paying taxes to Caesar, the cleansing of the temple. Truth, justice, strength of purpose and clear teaching are hallmarks of Jesus' ministry.

The pitfall thinkers need to watch out for is that in their passion for justice and a reasoned theology, they may not connect with the softer parts of themselves which need God's compassion and gentleness.

If you recognise in yourself a thinking preference, stand tall with it! We need Christians who can hold forth truth and stand up for justice. We need a thoughtful theology and an assertive proclamation of the gospel that makes sense to those who ask the hard questions. But don't leave your feelings out in the cold. Let God enrich your life through that channel too.

A heartfelt relationship (F)

'Were not our hearts burning within us?' (Luke 24:32).

For people with a feeling preference, a spirituality that is personal and relational is essential. Finding harmony with God and with others is a primary focus. A feeling person needs an environment of acceptance and love in order to trust and to grow. Intimacy with God is a great desire for a feeling person, but they often have a strong sense of their own inadequacy and failures.

Affirmation of God's forgiving love, and encouragement to see themselves as God sees them, is important for the spiritual journey of the feeler. That journey is a very personal journey with many ups and downs. Spiritual companionship and friendship are important. They need prayer to be an honest, open chance to share everything with God and to hear his personal response. Putting themselves in the biblical stories is one helpful way to do this. Keeping a journal where conversations with God can be recorded is another.

The gift of a feeling person is their capacity to enter deeply into relationships, both with God and with others. As they accept more and more deeply God's love for them, they are able to share it with those around them.

It is wonderful that the God we worship is a personal God. Our God initiates relationship with us through Jesus and calls us his beloved children. This is amazing. Many other belief systems have a remote God who is feared and respected, but not one who loves and is loved in return. To use the words of Jeremiah, 'The Lord is good; his love endures for ever' (Jeremiah 33:11). Jesus is the supreme example of God's concern for personal relationship. He lived right in the midst of his disciples. He was their constant companion, encouraging, affirming, challenging them. Jesus also modelled for them a life where emotion was allowed to show. We see Jesus weeping, angry, fearful, needing his friends with him in the garden, and in deep anguish. We also see him deeply appreciating personal care from others such as the anointing of his feet by women – and enjoying himself in feasting and partying.

A pitfall for a feeling person is that they may avoid discomfort by steering clear of things that are painful or challenging. Another common difficulty is that they think that feelings must always be stirred for prayer to be valid.

If you have a feeling preference, treasure it! Allow the full range of your feelings to be expressed to God, and receive fully his wise and loving responses. Use your capacity for empathy to relate to others with the acceptance and compassion of Jesus. We need a church which is a place of welcome not judgement. Strengthen those thinking muscles too, and let the unchanging truth of God's Word hold you steady when emotions tend to swamp your objectivity.

A disciplined relationship (J)

'All things should be done decently and in order' (1 Corinthians 14:40).

Some of the characteristics of a person with a judging preference are that they need a structure and an orderly way of approaching things. (By the way, 'judging' in this context doesn't mean judgemental, but desiring decisions and closure. To avoid the connotations we have around the word judging, I will use the letter J instead of repeating the word!) J's like clear boundaries and a sense of 'knowing where they are going'. They are very loyal to a group and will stick faithfully with any programme to which they have committed themselves.

Generally, J's will have a planned time for prayer and will probably have a routine they follow. They are good at being disciplined and managing their time, and will be committed to the devotional plan they have chosen to use. They may have prayer lists that divide up issues for prayer over the days of the week so that nothing is missed.

In public settings, J's will expect careful planning and an orderly approach to worship or Bible study. Too much 'letting things happen' will irritate them and feel like a waste of time. Of course, if a J is the one responsible for organising some aspect of group activity or public worship, it will be done efficiently and well. When it comes to church life, a sense of structure, organisation and appropriate discipline is clearly important. Groups of people cannot work well together without structure.

The gift of a J is their discipline and loyalty. They are people you can count on to be faithful.

The very creation of the world tells us that God is a God of structure and order. In creation he brought order out of chaos, which is often what J's feel they are doing! And God continually offers to bring order into the chaos of our lives and the world. Jesus wanted faithful, committed disciples. Sometimes he was saddened at how little loyalty they had. He himself modelled a commitment to his purpose on this earth even when it took him to dark and difficult places, ending in death.

A pitfall J's need to watch out for is that they may stay faithfully plodding along in an unhelpful rut. They may miss some of God's surprises by not expecting anything outside the structure they are used to.

If you have a judging preference, value it! Find spiritual disciplines that give you clear directions for your growth. Recognise that your role in the Christian community may be to provide structure and organisational skills. But be open to surprises too! Explore some new, less travelled pathways and find God there.

A spontaneous relationship (P)

'The wind blows where it chooses' (John 3:8).

People with a perceptive preference are open to new experiences, new paths. They want to be ready for surprises and like being flexible so they don't miss anything. Generally, perceptive people are comfortable with letting things happen according to the need or the ambience of the moment. They are often willing to risk and are ready to 'fly by the seat of their pants'.

They are likely to enjoy interacting with God in that way, too, rather than being too organised about their prayer. The phrase 'as the spirit leads' is one they relate to in a general sense, as well as in its strictly Christian meaning! Jesus was saying exactly that to Nicodemus.(John 3) You can't pin down everything about the way God works. God's Spirit is often going to come in surprising ways that break through our plans and boundaries.

In public worship, P's will feel at home in settings where there is room for that unforeseen movement of the Spirit. Charismatic and Pentecostal congregations usually expect that to happen and make room for it. But freedom to welcome the unexpected work of the Spirit is not limited to any denomination.

The gift of the perceptive person is just that: he or she is perceptive, likely to notice what is happening right now and flexible enough to respond to it.

God is a God of both order and surprises! Our God of order knows that sometimes we need to be blown out of our ruts by the wind of the Spirit. The New Testament is full of teaching about being set free from legalism and open to the surprises of life indwelt by the Spirit. Jesus modelled a flexible openness to the leading of the Spirit, and this shocked the Pharisees who were loyally committed to the 'way we've always done it'. Jesus travelled totally new territory, living out his relationship with God in ways no one else had done. His inner ear was tuned to the nudges of the Spirit right now for each situation.

A pitfall for perceptive people is that they may eagerly follow so many new paths that they don't go deep in any of them. They may also use spontaneity as an excuse to avoid discipline.

If you see in yourself a perceptive preference, enjoy its flexibility! Be alert to the still, small voice of the Spirit and be ready to respond. Enjoy the adventure of never knowing what might happen next. But remember that some of God's treasures are found only with disciplined attention and by sticking around long enough to mine the depths.

Enjoying the rainbow

Now I invite you to weave together the colours of your personality and see the whole pattern. There are probably four colours of the rainbow that you feel most at home with. Read them again, putting them together to see the combined 'giftedness' of your personality through which God's light shines. Be grateful for the personality God has given you, and the ways he meets you as you are.

Now read again the sections that represent colours you are less familiar with. Is there one or more that you are ready to explore more fully? Ask God to show you how. Seek out people who show that colour clearly in their own personality and ask them about it. Read books that expand on ways of praying you want to develop. You may want to revisit some of the earlier chapters of this book now that you understand more clearly why you found some ways of praying easy and others more challenging.

The further we travel on the journey with God, the more likely it is that all the colours become woven into our relationship. Even as I've been writing this chapter, I've noticed that, while still recognising the ways I most naturally relate to God, there are other colours firmly woven into our relationship now – and I wouldn't be without them! There is potential for all of us to have a relationship with God that is both active and reflective, that balances the down-to-earthness and the mystery of our faith, that meets God in thoughtful and heartfelt ways, and knows when to be disciplined and when to be spontaneous.

Keep exploring! It's a lifelong adventure. Let God go on creating the colourful tapestry of your life as you open yourself to his infinite resources.

Postscript
Staying deeply rooted

I wonder *how* you've read this book? Let me make a few guesses. Some of you will have read it methodically, chapter by chapter, noting the practical prayer suggestions and thinking you'll come back and try them later. Others may have browsed and skimmed some chapters and settled in to focus more fully on others that interested you more. I hope there will have been some of you who have stayed with each chapter long enough to actually enter prayerfully into the meditations and to try out the other ways of prayer in your daily life. There might even be a few of you who are right now reading the back page first before starting at the beginning!

Probably, you wouldn't even have picked up this book if you didn't have some desire to deepen your prayer life. So the question now is how you plan to stay 'planted by the water' so that your spiritual roots can continue to be nourished. The answer will be different for each person. If you are one of those who read the book and planned to come back to the meditations later, later has arrived! Choose a chapter that invites you in and take as many days – or weeks – as you need to truly *pray* through it. Then do the same with another chapter, and so on.

If you have already prayed your way through each chapter of this book, you now have some experience of several ways of meditating on scripture and of integrating meditative prayer into your active life. Your challenge is to find your own ongoing pattern and rhythm. Your personality will influence this to some extent. Do you need a disciplined structure of a certain time each day? Or do you find it more fruitful to take longer spaces now and then to go deeper than you can in a shorter, daily time? There's no 'right' and 'wrong' about this! Ask God's Spirit to help you discern the best way for you.

Some of you may have found some chapters really met you where you were and others didn't. That's OK! As we travel the spiritual journey, we have different needs at different times. Sink your roots deeply into the ways of prayer that nourish you right now, and don't feel guilty or anxious about those that don't. Trust that God will gently nudge you towards other ways of praying when the time is right.

You may want to look for other resources to guide your reading of scripture and prayerful meditation. Scripture Union offers many such resources. One of these, *Closer to God*, particularly encourages a creative and meditative approach to scripture.

There's one thing I know for sure: if you really want to follow the signpost to deep, nourishing, prayerful places, you will find a way. But be warned! The temptation to sit under the signpost and say, 'Maybe another day...' is very attractive. Keep your eyes on Jesus, who beckons you to fullness of life and truth, and who accompanies you on the way.

About
Closer to God

It's amazing but true that reading the Bible regularly and expecting God by his Holy Spirit to speak through it can empower us all to live more like Jesus and to do the things he did. And *Closer to God* is written and put together by a team whose heart's desire is to help make that happen in your life.

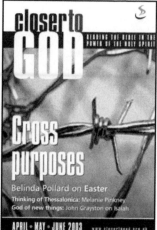

Closer to God is for anyone who longs to hear God's voice in today's noisy world. If you believe or hope that God speaks to ordinary people; loving, freeing, changing and healing them, then *Closer to God* is for you.

Each issue contains three months of material and variety is key. For every week you'll find:

A scene-setting introduction.

Five main Bible readings with notes. Usually these form part of a comprehensive exploration of the bible, but each issue also carries several theme weeks. A 'Bible in a year' plan at the foot of each note can be started at any time.

A meditation called Going deeper – a more experiential approach to a Bible theme raised during the week.

Looking outwards – a practical challenge for how to live out the Bible truths you've been examining in the real world.

Two extra readings with shorter notes. If you read the Bible every day these will fit into Saturday and Sunday, but if you don't have time to include these, the overall sense of the week's readings won't be affected.

There's also a magazine section called **UPclose**, with a range of articles on spirituality, the Closer to God team of writers, and the broader work of Scripture Union. In addition, each issue contains a colour bookmark with a Bible verse – yours to tear out and use to mark your place.

Closer to God

Reading the Bible in the power of the Holy Spirit

Closer to God is experiential, relational, radical and dynamic. This quarterly publication provides a uniquely creative and reflective approach to Bible reading with an emphasis on renewal. Every day of the week has a Bible reading with notes, but each weekly section is designed so that if you miss up to two days you still won't get behind.

185x127mm pb 128pp £2.75
Annual subscription £10

**Phone for your FREE *Closer to God* sampler today on
01908 856006**

Available from Scripture Union:
* by phone: 01908 856006
* by fax: 01908 856020
* by email: mailorder@scriptureunion.org.uk
* online: www.scriptureunion.org.uk
* by post: Scripture Union (Mail Order),
  PO Box 5148, Milton Keynes MLO, MK2 2YX
* through your church Bible reading representative.
* through your local Christian bookshop

**Hear God, get refreshed, be inspired.
Come on in! Get... *Closer to God*.**

So who is this man?

'Twenty-one centuries after he walked the dusty roads of Palestine, he is still famous around the world. Our dating system pivots around the year of his birth. Every day in homes and pubs and offices around the globe, people quote and misquote him, use his name as a swear word and argue about his significance...'

Closer to God for Newcomers:

Meet the Real Jesus

Written by popular *Closer to God* writer Belinda Pollard, *Closer to God for Newcomers* offers an encounter with Jesus through the Bible. It includes forty brief insights into biblical material describing Jesus' life, and the effect he had on the people he met. It is straightforward and jargon-free – readers don't need to know anything about Christianity to read it. Ideal for seekers and new Christians (Alpha and post-Alpha).

B format pb 98pp £2.65
1 85999 459 8

Pack of ten £19.50
1 85999 577 2

Dangerous Praying

David Spriggs

Could your prayer life be more adventurous? Are you willing to take risks, to expect great things from a great God? Drawing on Paul's letter to the Ephesians, this book is packed with practical ideas and strategies to help us develop a dynamic prayer life, whether individually or in a group.

B format pb 160pp £6.99

1 85999 335 4

Pack of 5 £24.95
1 85999 490 3

Multi-sensory Prayer

Sue Wallace

Over 60 innovative ideas to help you meet God in active, experiential prayer! Many Christians today are rediscovering the wealth of prayer techniques from across the Christian tradition and this fascinating resource provides a rich variety of creative ideas to revitalise prayer at church or in your small group. A photocopiable resource.

'I can see it being used in all kinds of contexts – church services, homegroups, personal devotions, retreats, with young people, in alternative worship. I'll certainly be using it!' Johnny Baker, Director of London Youth for Christ

A4 pb 64pp £7.99
1 85999 465 2

Multi-sensory Church

Sue Wallace

A follow up to the bestselling *Multi-sensory Prayer*, this photocopiable book is full of innovative ideas including meditations, liturgical prayers, imaginatively retold Bible stories, interactive labyrinths and prayer installations that will help transform your church service in a truly multi-sensory experience.

A4 pb 64pp £7.99
1 85999 667 1

How to Pray when Life Hurts (revised)

Roy Lawrence

This wonderful, practical book on prayer now contains three extra chapters.

It explains how to pray when going through difficult situations like illness or bereavement, or when feelings of guilt, anxiety, fear or anger get in the way.

Ideal both for personal use or to give to a friend.

B format pb 144pp £6.99
1 85999 674 4

Ready to Grow:
Practical steps to knowing God better

Allan Harkness

This practical book includes chapters on getting started, sharing what you have learned and different methods of combining Bible reading and prayer. Not just for the beginner – this book has much to offer the Christian looking for some fresh approaches to a walk with God.

188x125mm pb 176pp £5.99
0 949720 71 2

Available from Scripture Union

- by phone: 01908 856006
- by fax: 01908 856020
- by email: mailorder@scriptureunion.org.uk
- online: www.scriptureunion.org.uk
- by post: Scripture Union (Mail Order),
  PO Box 5148, Milton Keynes MLO, MK2 2YX
- through your local Christian bookshop